Women in India

The Problem of *Missing* Girl Child

Women in India

The Problem of *Missing* Girl Child

By

Nishant Anand

Advocate, Supreme Court of India

New Century Publications

New Delhi, India

NEW CENTURY PUBLICATIONS
4800/24, Bharat Ram Road,
Ansari Road, Daryaganj,
New Delhi - 110 002 (India)

Tel.: 011-2324 7798, 4358 7398, 6539 6605
Fax: 011-4101 7798
E-mail: indiatax@vsnl.com • info@newcenturypublications.com
www.newcenturypublications.com

Editorial office:
LG–7, Aakarshan Bhawan,
4754-57/23, Ansari Road, Daryaganj,
New Delhi – 110 002

Tel.: 011-4356 0919

First Published: **2016**

ISBN: **978-81-7708-419-1**

Published by New Century Publications and printed at Salasar Imaging Systems, New Delhi.

Designs: Patch Creative Unit, New Delhi.

PRINTED IN INDIA

About the Book

Advancement and empowerment of women has been a leading objective of state policy in India ever since the attainment of Independence in 1947. The principle of gender equality is enshrined in the Indian Constitution in its Preamble, Fundamental Rights, Fundamental Duties and Directive Principles of State Policy. The Constitution not only grants equality to women, but also empowers the state to adopt measures of positive discrimination in favour of women.

Gender equality is a constituent of development as well as an instrument of development. No country can be deemed developed if half of its population is severely disadvantaged in terms of basic needs, livelihood options, access to knowledge and political voice. A natural corollary of ensuring gender equality is the elimination of gender discrimination.

The problem of *missing* girl child pertains to unborn girl children in their mothers' wombs, who are deliberately disposed of (in contravention of the existing laws) before birth only because they are females. Their disposal before birth is extreme instance of gender discrimination, forbidden both by domestic and international laws and conventions.

The burgeoning size of this *missing* group is now receiving attention as a factor crucial to the health of the social fabric and to the well-being of communities.

2011 Census data shows that the sex ratio for children below 6 years (i.e. number of girls for every 1,000 boys) dropped from 927 in 2001 to a dismal 914 in 2011. This decline is unabated since 1961 Census.

This book provides deep insights into the problem of female foeticide in India. It explains and examines the reasons for its rapid growth, laws to safeguard the rights of women and the landmark judgments of courts in this context. Role of civil society and media has also been highlighted in improving the status of Indian women.

About the Author

Nishant Anand is a practicing advocate at the Supreme Court of India and the High Court of Delhi. He graduated from Vivekananda Institute of Professional Studies (Guru Gobind Singh Indraprastha University), Delhi. His key areas of practice include service laws, labor and industrial laws and matrimonial laws. He is a member of the Bar Association of India; Supreme Court Bar Association and Delhi High Court Bar Association.

Contents

Preface

Women play a critical role in the family which is the basic unit of a society. Family is a strong force for social cohesion and integration and as such should be strengthened. The inadequate support to women and insufficient protection to their respective families affect society as a whole and undermines efforts to achieve gender equality. In different cultural, political and social systems, various forms of families exist and the rights, capabilities and responsibilities of family members must be respected. Women's social and economic contribution to the welfare of the family continues to be inadequately addressed.

Advancement and empowerment of women has been a leading objective of the state policy in India ever since the attainment of Independence in 1947. Institutions of different types—Central, State and Local Governments, non-governmental organisations (NGOs), civil society and other bodies—are active to ensure gender equality as laid down in the Constitution of India.

The principle of gender equality is enshrined in the Indian Constitution in its Preamble, Fundamental Rights, Fundamental Duties and Directive Principles of State Policy. The Constitution not only grants equality to women, but also empowers the State to adopt measures of positive discrimination in favour of women.

Gender equality is a constituent of development as well as an instrument of development. No country can be deemed developed if half of its population is severely disadvantaged in terms of basic needs, livelihood options, access to knowledge, and political voice. It is an instrument of development because without gender equality, other goals of development will also be difficult to achieve, namely the goals of poverty alleviation, economic growth, environmental sustainability etc. A natural corollary of ensuring gender equality is the elimination of gender discrimination. Inequalities between girls and boys in access to schooling or adequate health care prove a very serious disadvantage to women and girls and limit their capacity to participate in the benefits of development.

The problem of *missing* girl child pertains to unborn girl children in their mothers' wombs, who are deliberately disposed of (in contravention of the existing laws) before birth only because they are females. Their disposal before birth is an extreme instance of gender discrimination, forbidden both by domestic and international laws and conventions.

The burgeoning size of this *missing* group is now receiving attention as a factor crucial to the health of the social fabric and to the well-being of communities. The high number of *missing* girls seriously affects the status of the living girls and women and their prospects for a safe and secure life.

Census 2011 data shows that the sex ratio for children below 6 years (i.e. number of girls for every 1,000 boys) dropped from 927 in 2001 to a dismal 914 in 2011. This decline is unabated since 1961 Census.

The problem of the *missing* girl child or the practice of female foeticide is not uncommon in India. The practice robs *missing* daughters not only of their right to healthy environment, good nutrition and education and the opportunity to reach their full potential, but also their right to birth. Gender has always shaped the legal and cultural landscapes of all countries. Of late, the graph of female foeticide in India is on the rise and the sex ratio gap is widening.

In India, feminine glory was at its zenith in the Vedic period, after which it suffered a decline. After Independence, the country enshrined not only the noble principles of equality, liberty and social justice but also provided for benign discrimination in favour of women in the Constitution of the country. The constitutional mandate was followed by the legislative intent being expressed in the form of various enactments which were passed to protect the rights and uphold the dignity of women.

However, despite the laws, discrimination and violence against women continues unabated. The malaise of female foeticide is reflected in a number of cases filed in various courts of the country. While women attempt to empower themselves economically, the girl child is being killed before she is born. The gender-sensitive approach of the judiciary, as reflected in a number of cases, is a ray of hope.

A sincere attempt has been made in this book to highlight the problem of female foeticide, reasons for its rapid growth, laws to safeguard the rights of women, and the landmark judgments of courts in this context. Role of civil society and media has also been highlighted in improving the status of Indian women.

Acknowledgements

I am grateful to the Almighty for giving me the courage to do, knowledge to understand and the will to attempt this work.

I place on record my deep sense of gratitude to Dr. Rajni Malhotra Dhingra for her support and guidance at every stage of the completion of this work.

Thanks are also due to Justice Veena Birbal, and Senior Advocates Mr. V. Shekhar, Mr. Navin Kumar Jaggi and Mrs. Sujatha Balachander for their help and inspiration to undertake this work.

I would also like to thank Mrs. Shilpa Khatri Babbar, Dean, External Relations and Protocol, Vivekananda Institute of Professional Studies (VIPS) and Dr. Rajni Malhotra Dhingra, Dean, Department of Law, VIPS for their support and co-operation.

Finally, I express my appreciation and regards for my family members, Mr. Narinder Kumar Anand (father), Mrs. Manjari Anand (mother) and Mr. Pratyush Anand (elder brother) for their moral support and encouragement during the course of writing this book.

New Delhi **Nishant Anand**

anand.nishant24@gmail.com

Abbreviations/Acronyms

AD	Anno Domini
AIR	All India Reporter
All.	Allahabad
asp	Active Server Pages
Bom.	Bombay
Cal.	Calcutta
CEDAW	Convention on Elimination of All Forms of Discrimination against Women
CRC	Convention on the Rights of the Child
Cri. LJ	Criminal Law Journal
FB	Full Bench
GDI	Gender Development Indices
GLR	Gujarat Law Report
http	Hypertext Transfer Protocol
ICPD	International Conference on Population and Development
IMR	Infant Mortality Rate
IPC	Indian Penal Code
Ker.	Kerala
MB	Madhya Bharat
MhLJ	Maharashtra Law Journal
MMR	Maternal Mortality Rate
MPLJ	Madhya Pradesh Law Journal
MPWN	Madhya Pradesh West Nimar
MTP	Medical Termination of Pregnancy Act, 1971
NGO	Non-governmental Organization
NPEW	National Policy on Empowerment of Women
NPP	National Population Policy
Ori.	Orissa
Para	Paragraph
PCPNDT	Pre-conception and Pre-natal Diagnostic Techniques (Regulation and Prevention of Misuse), Act
pdf	Portable Document Format

PH	Punjab and Haryana
PNDT	Pre-natal Diagnostic Techniques (Regulation and Prevention of Misuse) Act, 1994
SCALE	Supreme Court Almanac
SCC	Supreme Court Cases
SHGs	Self-help Groups
UN	United Nations
UOI	Union of India
US	United States
Utr.	Uttaranchal
www	World Wide Web

[illegible] Section 315—Act Done with Intent to Prevent Child Being Born Alive or to Cause it to Die after Birth: Whoever before the birth of any child does any act with the intention of thereby preventing the child from being born alive or causing it to die after its birth, and does by such act prevent that child from being born alive, or causes it to die after its birth, shall, if such act be not caused in good faith for the purpose of saving the life of the mother, be punishable with imprisonment of either description for a term which may extend to ten years, or with fine, or with both.

This Section is aimed at foeticide while in the womb after the foetus develops sufficiently to assume the human form which it does in normal cases in the sixth month. When it attains that degree of development the act which would, if done earlier, be abortion, ceases to be so as the delivery of an undeveloped child would be premature labour, for which the accused is held more responsible owing to more advanced stage of foetal life.

In spite of claiming ourselves to be an ancient civilized and cultured society, it is found that even in many well educated and wealthy families, female child is not welcomed with open arms. Unfortunately, the new technology is being used to perpetuate gender bias. For example, in recent past pre-natal diagnostic centres have mushroomed throughout the country [illegible] which help in determining sex of the foetus that enable people to choose to abort female foetus. Indian parents still believe that having a daughter is like watering someone else's field.

The tentacles of pre-natal diagnostic centres are no more confined to urban areas and cities.

'Mobile killer clinics' have reached even to remote rural areas. [illegible] mobile clinics conduct sex-determination tests for sums ranging between ₹ [illegible] and earn huge money [illegible]

1

Women in Indian Society

Advancement and empowerment of women has been a leading objective of state policy in India ever since the attainment of Independence in 1947. Institutions of different types—Central, state and local governments, non-governmental organisations (NGOs), civil society and other bodies—are active to ensure gender equality, as laid down in the Constitution of India.

The principle of gender equality is enshrined in the Indian Constitution in its Preamble, Fundamental Rights, Fundamental Duties and Directive Principles of State Policy. The Constitution not only grants equality to women, but also empowers the State to adopt measures of positive discrimination in favour of women. Since Independence in 1947, there has been a marked shift in the approach to issues related to welfare, development and empowerment of women. Within the framework of a democratic polity, India's laws, development policies, schemes/programmes under Five Year Plans, have aimed at advancement of women in different spheres. In recent years, the empowerment of women has been recognized as the central issue in determining the status of women. The National Commission for Women was set up by an Act of Parliament in 1990 to safeguard the rights and legal entitlements of women. The 73rd and 74th Amendments to the Constitution of India provided for reservation of seats for women in panchayats and municipalities, laying a strong foundation for their participation in decision-making at the local level.

India has also ratified various international conventions and human rights instruments committing to secure equal rights for women. Key among them is the ratification of the Convention on Elimination of All Forms of Discrimination against Women (CEDAW) in 1993.

The Mexico Plan of Action (1975), the Nairobi Forward

Looking Strategies (1985), the Beijing Declaration as well as the Platform for Action (1995) and the Outcome Document—adopted by the General Assembly Session of the United Nations on Gender Equality and Development and Peace for the 21st Century—titled "Further Actions and Initiatives to Implement the Beijing Declaration and the Platform for Action", have been unreservedly endorsed by India for appropriate follow up.

1.1 Role of Women in the Society

Women play a critical role in the family which is the basic unit of a society. Family is a strong force for social cohesion and integration and as such should be strengthened. The inadequate support to women and insufficient protection to their respective families affect the society as a whole and undermines efforts to achieve gender equality. In different cultural, political and social systems, various forms of family exist and the rights, capabilities and responsibilities of family members must be respected. Women's social and economic contributions to the welfare of the family and the social significance of maternity and paternity continue to be inadequately addressed. Motherhood and fatherhood and the role of parents and legal guardians in the family and in the upbringing of children and the importance of all family members to the family's well-being is also acknowledged and must not be a basis for discrimination. Women also continue to bear a disproportionate share of the household responsibilities and the care of children, the sick and the elderly. In order to achieve full partnership—both in public and private spheres—both women and men must be enabled to reconcile and share equally, the work and the family responsibilities.

Strong national machineries for the advancement of women and promotion of gender equality require political commitment at the highest level. Reforms to meet the challenges of the changing world are essential to ensure women's equal access to institutions and organizations. Institutional and conceptual changes are a strategic and important aspect of creating an enabling environment for the implementation of policies and programmes for the advancement of women.

Programme support to enhance women's opportunities, potentials and activities need to have a dual focus: on the one hand, programmes aimed at meeting the basic as well as the specific needs of women for capacity building, organizational development and empowerment; and on the other, gender mainstreaming in all programme formulation and implementation activities. It is particularly important to expand into new areas of programming to advance gender equality in response to current challenges.

Girls and women of all ages with any form of disability are generally among the more vulnerable and marginalized of the society. There is, therefore, need to take into account and to address their concerns in all policy-making and programming. Special measures are needed at all levels to integrate them into the mainstream of development.

Effective and coordinated plans and programmes for the full implementation of women-oriented policies require a clear knowledge on the situation of women and girls, a clear research-based knowledge and data disaggregated by sex, short and long-term time-bound targets and measurable goals and follow-up mechanisms to assess the progress. Efforts are needed to ensure capacity building for all the actors involved in the achievement of these goals. Efforts are also needed at the national level to increase transparency and accountability.

The realization of the goals of gender equality needs to be supported by the allocation of necessary human and financial resources for specific and targeted activities to ensure gender equality at the local, national, regional and international level as well as by enhanced and increased international cooperation. The explicit attention to these goals in budgetary processes at the national, regional and international level is essential.

Recognizing the persistent and increasing burden of poverty on women in many countries, particularly in developing countries, it is essential to continue from a gender perspective to review, modify and implement integrated macro-economic and social policies and programmes to ensure universal and equitable access to social services, in particular to education, and affordable quality health care services and equal access to and control over economic resources.

1.2 Need for Gender Equality

Gender equality is a constituent of development as well as an instrument of development. No country can be deemed developed if half of its population is severely disadvantaged in terms of basic needs, livelihood options, access to knowledge, and political voice. It is an instrument of development because without gender equality, other goals of development will also be difficult to achieve, namely the goals of poverty alleviation, economic growth, environmental sustainability etc. A natural corollary of ensuring gender equality is the elimination of gender discrimination. Inequalities between girls and boys in access to schooling or adequate health care prove a very serious disadvantage to women and girls and limit their capacity to participate in the benefits of development.

While the gender sensitization of policies, programmes and schemes go a long way in empowering women, it is human development indicators, which reflect the ultimate and true empowerment of women in a country. Unfortunately, the basic parameters of health (sex ratio, IMR, MMR, immunization levels, morbidity, mortality, anaemia etc.), nutrition (malnutrition, underweight, anaemia etc.), education, (illiteracy, poor enrolment, drop out etc.) employment and training (unorganised, unpaid sectors, discrimination in wages, poor skill development, drudgery areas of occupations such as agriculture and construction) reflect the continuing dismal status of women in various parts of the world.

1.3 Women in Modern India

The Constitution of the Republic of India ensures equality

for women and men in every sphere of life and activity. Women in India have been given equality of opportunity in all matters relating to education, employment, and legal status, and they can aspire to grace the highest offices of the State. However, this is indicative of the existing position of women in general in the country. Though legally and constitutionally all women have equal access to and right to venture in every walk of life, a vast majority of them are still illiterate and uneducated. This is a paradoxical situation which must be understood and seen in its historical perspective. The status of women and their activities can be divided into three main historical periods, the ancient, the medieval and the modern.

In the modern period, the status of Indian women can be divided into two distinct periods, the British Rule, i.e. Pre-Independence India and Post-Independence India.

1.3.1 Pre-Independence Period: The British Rule in the 18th century brought in some degree of political orderliness, but the social structure, customs and practices remained unchanged. It was mainly during the 19th century that the reform movement undertaken by enlightened thinkers and leaders of Indian society understood the importance of women's participation that the status of Indian women started changing for the better. Though initially all the leaders were men, women gradually came into the scene and played their role not only in changing history but also the society as a whole, through their efforts in different areas of work such as education, politics, freedom movement and social welfare. Annie Besant, Sarojini Naidu, Kamladevi Chattopadhyay, Nellie Sengupta, and many others gave a direction to Indian womanhood towards change and betterment. Indian women actively participated in the freedom movement which also had different thrusts and ideologies.

The founding of the Indian National Congress in 1885 and Mahatma Gandhi's non-violent movement not only led to political emancipation but also to social and national reconstruction. Women took equal initiatives and participated in all types of struggle for freedom, i.e. non-violent movement advocated by Mahatma Gandhi and the National Congress, as well as in the violent and armed movements advocated by other leaders in different parts of the country. Women's enthusiasm in participating in the armed revolution helped Netaji Subhash Chandra Bose to set up the Rani of Jhansi Regiment of the Indian National Army. Women's participation in the freedom movement was so extensive that the achievers are many in number. Some names of great significance are Kasturba Gandhi, Madam Bhikaji Cama, Sarla Devi, Muthu Lakshmi Reddy, Aruna Asaf Ali, Sucheta Kriplani, Durga Bai Deshmukh, Priti Lata Waddedar, Captain Lakshmi and Janaki Davar of INA, Jahanara Shahnawaz, and Randhabai Subbarayan.

1.3.2 Post-Independence Period: In 1947, India won freedom from foreign rule. In 1949, a Constitution was drafted which gave equal rights and status to all Indian citizens. Independent India has seen various reforms and programmes for the uplift of women of all communities. Indian women have played an important role from the very beginning of Independence in different walks of life. Women have taken bold steps in all nation-building activities, which started with education and have now blossomed into women's involvement in every activity of India. They have participated in all activities such as education, politics, media, art and culture, services sector and science and technology.

1.4 National Population Policy (NPP), 2000

The alarming growth of India's population calls for a systematic and effective population policy to curb the undesirable trend. The post-Independence population explosion has nullified, to a large extent, the gains of developmental efforts.

The policy of the Government of India to control population has relied excessively on family planning programme. Ever since the launching of the First Five Year Plan (1951-56), family planning has occupied an important place in the development strategy of the Government. Successive plans have allocated more and more resources for the implementation of family planning schemes. In 1966, a separate Department of Family Planning was created in the Union Ministry of Health. However, the results have not been encouraging.

Such dizzying rate of population growth negates whatever gains the nation has been able to achieve in agriculture, industrial and services sectors. Also, this leads to an unbearable burden on health, education, and housing sectors. If this trend is not halted, it will never be possible to render social and economic justice to millions of our masses. The current rate of population growth is simply not sustainable. In nutshell, the population explosion has proved a damper on the developmental efforts of the economy.

National Population Policy (NPP), 2000 outlined the long-term objective of attaining a stable population by 2045, a level consistent with the requirements of sustainable economic growth, social development and environment protection. Apart from implementation of the National Population Policy involving all social sector programmes, the State Governments too will have to play an important role in improving the social, economic and demographic indicators especially in the high fertility regions. In the long-run, it is necessary to have an explicit demographic vision of attaining less than half percent annual growth rate of population by the end of next decade. This would involve significant upgradation of the status of women in the society and attainment of almost 100 percent literacy among adult females.

NPP, 2000 also addressed issues of ensuring universal access to health care options and stabilising population. It recognised links between socio-economic development and health. The hallmark of India's National Population Policy is its emphasis on improving the quality of reproductive health care by working more closely with community-based organisations and women's groups. The policy provides a framework for advancing goals and prioritising strategies to meet the reproductive and child health needs of the people of India and to achieve net replacement levels of total fertility rate by 2010. The immediate objective of the policy is to address the unmet needs of contraception, health infrastructure, health personnel and to provide integrated service delivery for basic reproductive and child health care.

Satisfactorily, the decadal growth of population at 21.34 percent between 1991 and 2001 was the sharpest decline in the rate of growth of population witnessed since Independence, with the average exponential growth rate declining from 2.14 percent per annum during the previous decade to 1.93 percent per annum. The declining trends indicate that the country is entering a phase of rapidly declining fertility in its process of demographic transition.

Population stabilisation is crucial for the achievement of the goal of sustainable development and an equitable distribution of resources/opportunities. Though Government initiatives exist in the form of suitable public policies on education, health and family welfare along with economic incentives and facilities for small and micro-families, these measures have had a limited impact on the fertility, net reproduction rates and the family size. Improved access to primary and secondary education extension of basic amenities, the empowerment of women, awareness generation and a better standard of living would ultimately contribute towards inculcation of the required consciousness regarding the desirability of a small family size.

1.5 National Policy for Empowerment of Women, 2001

Progress towards gender equality and women's empowerment in India has been built upon strong commitments by the government and unflagging effort by the women's movement. India's commitment to gender equality is further evidenced by the fact that it is a signatory to Convention on the Elimination of All Forms of Discrimination against Women (CEDAW), which was ratified on June 25, 1993 (with one reservation and two declaratory statements). India is also a signatory to the Convention on the Rights of the Child. The first report to the UN Committee of Experts on the Rights of the Child was submitted in 2000 and the second report in 2004.

In pursuance of the avowed objective of empowering the *women* as agents of socio-economic change, the National Policy on Empowerment of Women (NPEW) was adopted in April 2001. Gender inequality arising out of social norms and cultural traditions has been addressed through a range of direct and indirect measures, and the aim of the NPEW has been to bring about social change—changes in attitudes towards women, and women's empowerment. The policy itself reflects the aspirations of women and the women's movement. The effort is to bring gender justice and make *de jure* equality into *de facto* equality. Several State Governments have also formulated a policy for women's empowerment.

On the basis of NPEW, the National Plan of Action is being implemented which includes the following strategies:

1. To create an enabling environment for women to exercise their rights both within and outside their homes.
2. To reserve one-third of seats for women in the Lok Sabha and State Legislative Assemblies.
3. To adopt a special strategy for Women Component Plan to ensure that at least 30 percent of funds and benefits flow to women from all development sectors.
4. To organize women in self-help groups as a mark of the beginning of empowering them.
5. To accord high priority and ensure easy access to maternal and child health services.
6. To initiate steps for eliminating gender bias in all educational programmes; further to institute plans for free education of girls up to college levels including professional levels.
7. To equip women with necessary skills in modern upcoming trades which would make them economically independent and self-reliant.
8. To increase women's access to credit through setting up of development bank for women entrepreneurs in small and tiny sectors.

Various aspects of NPEW are as under.

1.5.1 Objectives of the Policy: National Policy for Empowerment of Women, 2001 was formulated for bringing about advancement, development and empowerment of women in all spheres of life through creation of a more responsive judicial and legal system sensitive to women and mainstreaming a gender perspective in the development process. The strengthening and formation of relevant institutional mechanisms and implementation of international obligations/commitments and co-operation at the international, regional and sub-regional level was another commitment.

The primary objective of NPEW was to bring about the advancement, development and empowerment of women. Specifically, the objectives of this Policy included the following:

1. Creating an environment through positive economic and social policies for full development of women to enable them to realize their full potential.
2. The *de-jure* and *de-facto* enjoyment of all human rights and fundamental freedom by women on equal basis with men in all spheres—political, economic, social, cultural and civil.
3. Equal access to participation and decision-making of women in social, political and economic life of the nation.
4. Equal access to women to healthcare, quality education at all levels, career and vocational guidance, employment, equal remuneration, occupational health and safety, social security and public office etc.
5. Strengthening legal systems aimed at elimination of all forms of discrimination against women.
6. Changing societal attitudes and community practices by active participation and involvement of both men and women.
7. Mainstreaming a gender perspective in the development process.
8. Elimination of discrimination and all forms of violence against women and the girl child.
9. Building and strengthening partnerships with civil society,

particularly women's organizations.

1.5.2 Politico-legal Empowerment of Women:

A. Legal-Judicial System: Legal-judicial system would be made more responsive and gender sensitive to women's needs, especially in cases of domestic violence and personal assault. New laws would be enacted and existing laws reviewed to ensure that justice is quick and the punishment meted out to the culprits is commensurate with the severity of the offence.

At the initiative of and with the full participation of all stakeholders including community and religious leaders, NPEW would aim to encourage changes in personal laws such as those related to marriage, divorce, maintenance and guardianship so as to eliminate discrimination against women.

The evolution of property rights in a patriarchal system has contributed to the subordinate status of women. NPEW would aim to encourage changes in laws relating to ownership of property and inheritance by evolving consensus in order to make them gender just.

B. Decision-making: Women's equality in power sharing and active participation in decision making, including decision-making in political process at all levels would be ensured for the achievement of the goals of empowerment. All measures would be taken to guarantee women equal access to and full participation in decision-making bodies at every level, including the legislative, executive, judicial, corporate, statutory bodies, as also the advisory commissions, committees, boards, trusts etc. Affirmative action such as reservations/quotas, including in higher legislative bodies, will be considered whenever necessary on a time-bound basis. Women-friendly personnel policies will also be drawn up to encourage women to participate effectively in the developmental process.

C. Mainstreaming a Gender Perspective in the Development Process: Policies, programmes and systems would be established to ensure mainstreaming of women's perspectives in all developmental processes, as catalysts, participants and recipients. Wherever there are gaps in policies and programmes, women-specific interventions would be undertaken to bridge these. Coordinating and monitoring mechanisms will also be devised to assess, from time to time, the progress of such mainstreaming mechanisms. Issues and concerns related to women would be specifically addressed and reflected in all concerned laws, sectoral policies, plans and programmes of action.

1.5.3 Economic Empowerment of Women:

A. Poverty Eradication: Since women comprise the majority of the population below the poverty line and are very often in situations of extreme poverty—given the harsh realities of intra-household and social discrimination—macro-economic policies and poverty eradication programmes would specifically address the needs and problems of such women. There would be improved implementation of programmes which are already women-oriented with special targets for women. Steps would be taken for mobilization of poor women and convergence of services, by offering them a range of economic and social options, along with necessary support measures to enhance their capabilities.

B. Micro Credit: In order to enhance women's access to credit for consumption and production, establishment of new and strengthening of existing micro-credit mechanisms and micro-finance institution would be undertaken so that the outreach of credit is enhanced. Other supportive measures would be taken to ensure adequate flow of credit through extant financial institutions and banks so that all women below poverty line have easy access to credit.

C. Women and Economy: Women's perspectives would be included in designing and implementing macro-economic and social policies by institutionalizing their participation in such processes. Their contribution to socio-economic development as producers and workers would be recognized in the formal and informal sectors (including home-based workers) and appropriate policies relating to employment and to her working conditions would be drawn up. Such measures could include the following:

1. Reinterpretation and redefinition of conventional concepts of work wherever necessary (e.g. in the census records), to reflect contribution of women as producers and workers.
2. Preparation of satellite and national accounts.
3. Development of appropriate methodologies for undertaking (1) and (2) above.

D. Globalization: Globalization—the gender impact of which has not been evaluated fully—has presented new challenges for the realization of the goal of women's equality. It is evident that there is a need for re-framing policies for access to employment and quality of employment.

Benefits of the growing global economy have been unevenly distributed leading to wider economic disparities, the feminization of poverty, increased gender inequality through deteriorating working conditions and unsafe working environment especially in the informal economy and rural areas. Strategies would be designed to enhance the capacity of women and empower them to meet the negative social and economic impacts, which may flow from the globalization process.

E. Women and Agriculture: In view of the critical role of women in the agriculture and allied sectors as producers, concentrated efforts would be made to ensure that benefits of various programmes/schemes reach them in proportion to their numbers. The programmes for training women in soil conservation, social forestry, dairy development and other occupations allied to agriculture (like horticulture, livestock including small animal husbandry, poultry, fisheries etc.) would be expanded to benefit women workers in the agriculture sector.

F. Women and Industry: The important role played by women in electronics, information technology, food processing, agro industry and textiles has been crucial for the development of these sectors. They would be given comprehensive support in terms of labour legislation, social security and other support services to participate in various industrial sectors.

Women at present cannot work in night shift in factories even if they wish to. Suitable measures will be taken to enable women to work on the night shift in factories. This would be accompanied with support services for security, transportation etc.

G. Support Services: The provision of support services for women—like child care facilities, including crèches at work places and educational institutions, homes for the aged and the disabled—would be expanded and improved to create an enabling environment and to ensure their full cooperation in social, political and economic life. Women-friendly personnel policies would also be drawn up to encourage women to participate effectively in the developmental process.

1.5.4 Social Empowerment of Women:

A. Education: Equal access to education for women and girls would be ensured. Special measures would be taken to eliminate discrimination, universalize education, eradicate illiteracy, create a gender-sensitive educational system, increase enrolment and retention rates of girls and improve the quality of education to facilitate life-long learning as well as development of occupation/vocation/technical skills by women. Reducing the gender gap in secondary and higher education would be a focus area. Sectoral time targets in existing policies would be achieved, with a special focus on girls and women, particularly those belonging to weaker sections including the scheduled castes/scheduled tribes/other backward classes/minorities. Gender sensitive curricula would be developed at all levels of educational system in order to address sex stereotyping as one of the causes of gender discrimination.

B. Health: A holistic approach to women's health which includes both nutrition and health services would be adopted and special attention would be given to the needs of women and the girls at all stages of the life cycle. The reduction of infant mortality and maternal mortality, which are sensitive indicators of human development, is a priority concern. NPEW reiterated the national demographic goals for infant mortality rate (IMR), maternal mortality rate (MMR) set out in the National Population Policy, 2000. Women should have access to comprehensive, affordable and quality health care. Measures .would be adopted that take into account the reproductive rights of women to enable them to exercise informed choices, their vulnerability to sexual and health problems together with endemic, infectious and communicable diseases such as malaria, TB, and water-borne diseases as well as hypertension and cardio-pulmonary diseases. The social, developmental and health consequences of HIV/AIDS and other sexually transmitted diseases would be tackled from a gender perspective.

To effectively meet problems of infant and maternal mortality, and early marriage, the availability of good and accurate data at micro level on deaths, birth and marriages is required. Strict implementation of registration of births and deaths would be ensured and registration of marriages would be made compulsory.

In accordance with the commitment of the National Population Policy, 2000 to population stabilization, NPEW recognized the critical need of men and women to have access to safe, effective and affordable methods of family planning of their choice and the need to suitably address the issues of early marriages and spacing of children. Interventions such as spread of education, compulsory registration of marriage should impact on delaying the age of marriage so that by 2010 child marriages are eliminated.

Women's traditional knowledge about health care and nutrition would be recognized through proper documentation and its use would be encouraged. The use of Indian and alternative systems of medicine would be enhanced within the framework of overall health infrastructure available for women.

C. Nutrition: In view of the high risk of malnutrition and disease that women face at all the three critical stages, viz.

infancy and childhood, adolescent and reproductive phase, focussed attention would be paid to meeting the nutritional needs of women at all stages of the life cycle. This is also important in view of the critical link between the health of adolescent girls, pregnant and lactating women with the health of infant and young children. Special efforts would be made to tackle the problem of macro and micro nutrient deficiencies, especially amongst pregnant and lactating women as it leads to various diseases and disabilities.

Intra-household discrimination in nutritional matters vis-à-vis girls and women would be sought to be ended through appropriate strategies. Widespread use of nutrition education would be made to address the issues of intra-household imbalances in nutrition and the special needs of pregnant and lactating women. Women's participation would also be ensured in the planning, superintendence and delivery of the system.

D. Drinking Water and Sanitation: Special attention would be given to the needs of women in the provision of safe drinking water, sewage disposal, toilet facilities and sanitation within accessible reach of households, especially in rural areas and urban slums. Women's participation would be ensured in the planning, delivery and maintenance of such services.

E. Housing and Shelter: Women's perspectives would be included in housing policies, planning of housing colonies and provision of shelter both in rural and urban areas. Special attention would be given for providing adequate and safe housing and accommodation for women including single women, heads of households, working women, students, apprentices and trainees.

F. Environment: Women would be involved and their perspectives reflected in the policies and programmes for environment, conservation and restoration. Considering the impact of environmental factors on their livelihoods, women's participation would be ensured in the conservation of the environment and control of environmental degradation. The vast majority of rural women still depend on the locally available non-commercial sources of energy such as animal dung, crop waste and fuel wood. In order to ensure the efficient use of these energy resources in an environmental friendly manner, NPEW would aim at promoting the programmes of non-conventional energy resources. Women would be involved in spreading the use of solar energy, biogas, smokeless chulahs and other rural application so as to have a visible impact of these measures in influencing eco system and in changing the life styles of rural women.

G. Science and Technology: Programmes would be strengthened to bring about a greater involvement of women in science and technology. These would include measures to motivate girls to take up science and technology for higher education and also ensure that development projects with scientific and technical inputs involve women fully. Efforts to develop a scientific temper and awareness would also be stepped up. Special measures would be taken for their training in areas where they have special skills like communication and information technology. Efforts to develop appropriate technologies suited to women's needs as well as to reduce their drudgery would be given a special focus too.

H. Women in Difficult Circumstances: In recognition of the diversity of women's situations and in acknowledgement of the needs of disadvantaged groups, measures and programmes would be undertaken to provide them with special assistance. These groups include women in extreme poverty, destitute women, women in conflict situations, women affected by natural calamities, women in less developed regions, the disabled widows, elderly women, single women in difficult circumstances, women heading households, those displaced from employment, migrants, women who are victims of marital violence, deserted women and prostitutes etc.

I. Violence against Women: All forms of violence against women, physical and mental, whether at domestic or societal levels, including those arising from customs, traditions or accepted practices shall be dealt with effectively with a view to eliminate its incidence. Institutions and mechanisms for assistance would be created and strengthened for prevention of such violence—including sexual harassment at workplace—and for the rehabilitation of the victims of violence and for taking effective action against the perpetrators of such violence. A special emphasis would also be laid on programmes and measures to deal with trafficking in women and girls.

J. Rights of the Girl Child: All forms of discrimination against the girl child and violation of her rights shall be eliminated by undertaking strong measures both preventive and punitive within and outside the family. These would relate specifically to strict enforcement of laws against prenatal sex selection and the practices of female foeticide, female infanticide, child marriage, child abuse and child prostitution etc. Removal of discrimination in the treatment of the girl child within the family and outside and projection of a positive image of the girl child would be actively fostered. There would be special emphasis on the needs of the girl child and earmarking of substantial investments in the areas relating to food and nutrition, health and education, and in vocational education. In implementing programmes for eliminating child labour, there would be a special focus on girl children.

K. Mass Media: Media would be used to portray images consistent with human dignity of girls and women. NPEW would specifically strive to remove demeaning, degrading and negative conventional stereotypical images of women and violence against women. Private sector partners and media networks would be involved at all levels to ensure equal access for women, particularly in the area of information and communication technologies. The media would be encouraged to develop codes of conduct, professional guidelines and other self-regulatory mechanisms to remove gender stereotypes and promote balanced portrayals of women and men.

1.5.5 Operational Strategies of NPEW

A. Action Plans: All Central and State Ministries would draw up time bound Action Plans for translating NPEW into a set of concrete actions, through a participatory process of consultation with Central/State Departments of Women and Child Development and National/State Commissions for Women. The Plans would specifically include the following:

1. Measurable goals to be achieved by 2010.
2. Identification and commitment of resources.
3. Responsibilities for implementation of action points.
4. Structures and mechanisms to ensure efficient monitoring, review and gender impact assessment of action points and policies.
5. Introduction of a gender perspective in the budgeting process.

In order to support better planning and programme formulation and adequate allocation of resources, gender development indices (GDI) would be developed by networking with specialized agencies. These could be analyzed and studied in depth. Gender auditing and development of evaluation mechanisms would also be undertaken along side.

Collection of gender disaggregated data by all primary data collecting agencies of the Central and State Governments as well as research and academic institutions in the public and private sectors would be undertaken. Data and information gaps in vital areas reflecting the status of women would be sought to be filled in by these immediately. All Ministries/Corporations/Banks and financial institutions etc. would be advised to collect, collate, disseminate and maintain/publish data related to programmes and benefits on a gender disaggregated basis. This would help in meaningful planning and evaluation of policies.

B. Institutional Mechanisms: Institutional mechanisms, to promote the advancement of women, which exist at the Central and State levels, would be strengthened. This would be done through appropriate and would relate to, among others, provision of adequate resources, training and skills to effectively influence macro-policies, legislations, programmes etc. to achieve the empowerment of women.

National and State Councils would be formed to oversee the operationalisation of the Policy on a regular basis. The National Council would be headed by the Prime Minister and the State Councils by the Chief Ministers and would be broad in composition having representatives from the concerned departments/ministries, national and state commissions for women, social welfare boards, representatives of non-government organizations, women's organisations, corporate sector, trade unions, financing institutions, academics, experts and social activists. These bodies would review the progress made in implementing the Policy twice a year. The National Development Council would also be informed, from time to time, of the progress of the programme undertaken under the policy for advice and comments.

National and state resource centres on women would be established with mandates for collection and dissemination of information, undertaking research work, conducting surveys, implementing training and awareness generation programmes etc. These centres would link up with women's studies centres and other research and academic institutions through suitable information networking systems.

While institutions at the district level would be strengthened, women would be helped by Government at the grassroots level through its programmes to organize and strengthen self-help groups (SHGs) at the anganwadi, village and town levels. The women's groups would be helped to institutionalize themselves into registered societies and to federate at the panchyat/municipal level. These societies would bring about synergistic implementation of all the social and economic development programmes by drawing resources made available through Government and non-government channels, including banks and financial institutions and by establishing a close interface with the panchayats/municipalities.

C. Resource Management: Availability of adequate financial, human and market resources to implement NPEW would be managed by concerned departments, financial credit institutions and banks, private sector, civil society and other connected institutions. This process would include the following:

1. Assessment of benefits flowing to women and resource allocation to the programmes relating to them through an exercise of gender budgeting. Appropriate changes in policies would be made to optimize benefits to women under these schemes.
2. Adequate resource allocation to develop and promote the policy outlined earlier based on (1) above by concerned departments.
3. Developing synergy between personnel of health, rural development, education and women and child development department at field level and other village level functionaries.
4. Meeting credit needs by banks and financial credit institutions through suitable policy initiatives and development of new institutions in coordination with the Department of Women and Child Development.

The strategy of Women's Component Plan adopted in the Ninth Five Year Plan (1997-98 to 2001-02) ensuring that not less than 30 percent of benefits/funds flow to women from all Ministries and Departments would be implemented effectively so that the needs and interests of women and girls are addressed by all concerned sectors. The Department of Women and Child Development being the nodal Ministry will monitor and review the progress of the implementation of the Component Plan from time to time in terms of both quality and quantity in collaboration with the Planning Commission.

Efforts would be made to channelize private sector investments also, to support programmes and projects for advancement of women.

D. Legislation: The existing legislative structure would be reviewed and additional legislative measures taken by identified departments to implement the Policy. This would also involve a review of all existing laws including personal, customary and tribal laws, subordinate legislation, related rules as well as executive and administrative regulations to eliminate all gender discriminatory references. The process would be planned over a time period 2000-03. The specific measures required would be evolved through a consultation process involving civil society, National Commission for Women, and Department of Women and Child Development. In appropriate cases, the consultation process would be widened to include other stakeholders also.

Effective implementation of legislations would be promoted by involving civil society and community. Appropriate changes in legislations would be undertaken, if necessary. In addition, following other specific measures would be taken to implement the legislation effectively:

1. Strict enforcement of all relevant legal provisions and speedy redressal of grievances would be ensured, with a special focus on violence and gender related atrocities.
2. Measures to prevent and punish sexual harassment at the place of work, protection for women workers in the organized/unorganized sector and strict enforcement of relevant laws such as Equal Remuneration Act and Minimum Wages Act would be undertaken.
3. Crimes against women, their incidence, prevention, investigation, detection and prosecution would be regularly reviewed at all crime review fora and conferences at the Central, State and District levels. Recognised, local, voluntary organizations would be authorized to lodge complaints and facilitate registration, investigations and legal proceedings related to violence and atrocities against girls and women.
4. Women's cells in police stations, women police stations, family courts, *mahila* courts, counselling centres, legal aid centres and *nyaya panchayats* would be strengthened and expanded to eliminate violence and atrocities against women.
5. Widespread dissemination of information on all aspects of legal rights, human rights and other entitlements of women,

through specially designed legal literacy programmes and rights information programmes would be done.

E. Gender Sensitization: Training of personnel of executive, legislative and judicial wings of the State—with a special focus on policy and programme framers, implementation and development agencies, law enforcement machinery and the judiciary, as well as non-governmental organizations—would be undertaken. Other measures would include the following:

1. Promoting societal awareness of gender issues and women's human rights.
2. Review of curriculum and educational materials to include gender education and human rights issues.
3. Removal of all references derogatory to the dignity of women from all public documents and legal instruments.
4. Use of different forms of mass media to communicate social messages relating to women's equality and empowerment.

F. Panchayati Raj Institutions: The 73rd and 74th Amendments to the Indian Constitution have served as a breakthrough towards ensuring equal access and increased participation of women in political power structure. The PRIs would play a central role in the process of enhancing women's participation in public life. The PRIs and the local self-governments would be actively involved in the implementation and execution of NPEW the grassroots level.

G. Partnership with the Voluntary Sector Organizations: The involvement of voluntary organizations, associations, federations, trade unions, non-governmental organizations, women's organizations, as well as institutions dealing with education, training and research would be ensured in the formulation, implementation, monitoring and review of all policies and programmes affecting women. Towards this end, they would be provided with appropriate support related to resources and capacity building and facilitated to participate actively in the process of the empowerment of women.

H. International Cooperation: NPEW would aim at implementation of international obligations/commitments in all sectors on empowerment of women such as the Convention on All Forms of Discrimination Against Women (CEDAW), Convention on the Rights of the Child (CRC), International Conference on Population and Development (ICPD) and other such instruments. International, regional and sub-regional cooperation towards the empowerment of women would continue to be encouraged through sharing of experiences, exchange of ideas and technology, networking with institutions and organizations and through bilateral and multi-lateral partnerships.

1.6 The *Missing* Girl Child

This group consists of the unborn girl children in their mothers' wombs, who are deliberately disposed of (in contravention of existing laws) before birth only because they are female. Their disposal is an instance of the most extreme instance of gender discrimination, (forbidden both by domestic and international laws and conventions), but seldom regarded as such, it being more commonly referred to as a social issue.

The burgeoning size of this *missing* group is now receiving attention as a factor crucial to the health of the social fabric and to the well-being of communities. The high numbers of missing girls seriously affect the status of the living girls and women and their prospects for a safe and secure life. Less realized is the strong possibility that increasing numbers of 'missing' girl children are also inimical to the safety and health (including mental and psychological health) of mothers. Repeated abortions weaken the reproductive health system and increase the risk of infections.

Women from lower socio-economic strata are also being trafficked from *supply centres* (e.g. Kerala) to *demand centres* (e.g. Haryana) to make up for the deficit of females in the marriageable age groups. All such women are treated as merchandise, as *inferior* wives and many of them are abandoned as soon they carry out their apportioned task of giving birth to children.

In *deficit areas*, there is also some evidence emerging of

increased surveillance over young girls and their physical movements at the village and local level, by traditional male-dominated councils such as the *khap panchayats*. The incidence of violence against women is on the rise, giving the lie to the myth that lesser numbers of women means better and more humane treatment, resulting in higher status.

Factors responsible for female foeticide are many, complex and interlinking. A succinct summarization is given below:

1. Obsession to have a son.
2. Discrimination against the girl child.
3. Socio-economic and physical insecurity of women.
4. Evil of dowry prevalent in our society.
5. Worry about getting girls married as there is the stigma attached to being an unmarried woman.
6. Easily accessible and affordable procedures for sex selection during pregnancy.
7. Failure of medical ethics.
8. Two-child norm policy of certain State Governments.

The two-child norm implies that the State promotes two children per family and has a system of incentives and disincentives/punishments for achieving it. A two child norm has the potential to cause immense harm to women's health in the existing social situation where son preference is high and women's status is very low. One of the gravest risks includes increase in sex selective abortion and consequent reduction in the numbers of girl children. The compulsion to have no more than two children would result in increased female foeticide. This happened in China when Government declared that no couple should have more than one child. There are lessons to be learnt from the Chinese experience.

There are two important issues of policy associated with the decline in the child sex ratio. One is the obsession with population control, which assumes that all the failures in development can be linked to population explosion. The other more recent issue is the intrusion of the two-child norm into the Panchayati Raj Acts of many States, leading to disqualification of many elected representatives. Most of the excluded belong to the SCs and STs. Some experts have suggested a link between the imposition of the two-child norm and sex selective abortions. Imposition of the two-child norm then cannot be the route to population stabilization, for it may lead to a disturbingly unbalanced population.

Women are victims of iniquitous gender relationships. If they fail to produce sons, they face desertion, humiliation and witch hunts. Yet, they are also deemed to be the wrong doers when they attempt to dispose of the female children in the foetal stage or in infancy. In almost all cases, this action is collaborative, taken in consultation with other family members, both male and female. In certain parts of the country, women are punished under the law for committing female infanticide and are imprisoned. The compulsions behind these acts by the women can be imagined. The act of giving birth to girls becomes a justified ground for abandonment of the mothers. In some cases, the *guilty* women themselves, opt out of the marriage, locating a sister or any close relation or a stranger to take her place, who would produce a child of the *right* gender.

Within the Government of India's Rules of Business, subjects such as women's physical and mental health, sex ratios, the two child norm, violence against women, population control and stabilization programs, trafficking and prostitution, child health and nutrition, abortion rights, female foeticide, child survival etc. do not fall neatly into the purview of one or the other government ministries or departments. A number of agencies (both at the central and state level) are responsible for these and other allied subjects. It is difficult to fix accountability for the safe survival, healthy development and well being of the girl child and the mother at a single point. Inter-agency coordination is the mechanism that is conventionally resorted to; yet, inter-agency coordination has been one of the weakest links in government working, where the system tends to function in hierarchies, leaving little space for lateral thinking or action. Plans of action for the girl child at national and regional levels, in which effective level coordination has been the key requirement, have therefore not been either successful or effective.

The entity of Girl Child was brought into public focus only since the late 1980s. Prior to this, a *gendered* view of childhood was seldom taken. Public agencies and most child lobbies saw childhood for both boys and girls as a uniformly vulnerable and critical period, when children needed the same levels and types of services such as nutrition, health care, education, cognitive stimulation, shelter, play opportunities etc. This general, non-gendered view remained predominant, even though data collected by researchers from the field did show that girls had less access to breast milk and were less often likely to be taken to public hospitals when ill as compared to boys.

Similarly, the girl child tended to remain invisible in the eyes of women's rights groups and women's development agencies. Here, the tendency was to identify *women* only in terms of adult age groups and to deal with patriarchal oppression and exploitation of women who had reached the child bearing age. In other words, the girl child fell between the two stools of age and gender and remained submerged. There were no separate planning provisions for the girl child either amongst children or amongst women. The gendered links with childhood or womanhood were also not apparent.

From the 1990s, MWCD has included the girl child on its agenda and in its programming and budget allocations. It has accepted that discrimination against the girl child is not merely a result of poverty and illiteracy, but is rooted in traditionally ingrained attitudes and mindset. The perspective that is now needed has to be a much larger one and has to take on board not only State Governments, but other organizations such as local bodies, media, medical doctors and lawyers etc. Also, MWCD has to play a continuous gender monitoring and auditing role in terms of keeping in touch with the field on the repercussions of coercive polices such as the two child norm and incentives and disincentives being offered by several State Governments in favour of this norm.

2

Vulnerable Groups of Women

Women are not homogenous categories. They belong to diverse castes, classes, communities, economic groups, and are located within a range of geographic and development zones. Consequently, some groups are more vulnerable than others. Mapping and addressing the specific deprivations that arise from these multiple locations is essential for the success of planned interventions. Thus, apart from the general programme interventions, special targeted interventions, catering to the differential needs of these groups, should be undertaken.

Policies, programmes and schemes for women are generally formulated as if they are comprised of one composite and homogenous group. In reality, there are many layers of heterogonous groups of women with differing degrees of vulnerabilities, depending on their socio-economic and geo-political backgrounds. Therefore, specific strategies and programmes need to be developed to address the unique problems of specific groups.

Amongst vulnerable groups, the women belonging to socially backward communities—such as scheduled castes (SCs), scheduled tribes (STs) and other backward classes (OBCs)—face double discrimination of being a woman and also from a backward community. Similarly, women with disabilities have specific problems even when compared to men with disability. There are women who are victims of violence or sexual abuse such as trafficked women, rape victims who need a very different but specialized rehabilitation package. Adolescent girls are a highly vulnerable group as they are subject to a number of atrocities like trafficking, rape, and child marriage. Child marriages are increasingly taking place and witch hunting is now increasingly linked not only to women's property rights but also to bigamy. Non-participation in the traditional decision-making forums, increase in the incidence of alcoholism and the resulting domestic violence are other problems of women.

The following illustrates a list of categories of women who are in difficult circumstances. These categories of women find themselves more vulnerable on account of their unique social, cultural circumstances or because they are victims of violence or abuse. These groups require special interventions to address their needs. The possibility of developing pilot projects suitably formulated to address specific requirements may be examined.

2.1 Women with Health Problems

2.1.1 Women Affected by HIV/AIDS: The rapid progression of the HIV/AIDS pandemic, particularly in the developing world, has had a devastating impact on women. Responsible behaviour and gender equality are among the important prerequisites for its prevention. There is also the need for more effective strategies to empower women to have control over and decide freely and responsibly on matters related to their sexuality, to protect themselves from high risk and irresponsible behaviour leading to sexually transmitted infections including HIV/AIDS and to promote responsible, safe and respectful behaviour by men and to also promote gender equality.

The burden of care for people living with HIV/AIDS and for children orphaned by HIV/AIDS falls particularly on women, as infrastructure is inadequate to respond to the challenges being posed. Women with HIV/AIDS often suffer from discrimination and a stigma and are often victims of violence.

2.1.2 Women with Disability: The 2001 Census estimated that there were over 9 million women with disabilities in India constituting 3.5 percent of the population. The majority of women with disabilities in India suffer the *triple discrimination of being female, being disabled* and *being poor*.

Indeed not only are they a socially invisible category but their plight is worse than both men with disabilities and other non-disabled women.

While being a man and being disabled are very incongruous, being female and being disabled also implies a certain level of continuity as both are to varying degrees associated with notions of weakness, passivity and dependence. But the likeness is only superficial because a disabled woman is also considered incapable of fulfilling the normative feminine roles of homemaker, wife and mother. Then, she also does not fit the stereotype of the normal woman in terms of physical appearance. Since women embody family honour, disabled girls are kept hidden at home by families and denied basic rights to mobility, education and employment. They are less likely to be given in marriage than disabled men.

Doubts around the capacity of women with disabilities to be sexual partners, homemakers and mothers abound. They are not considered capable of performing household chores efficiently, having meaningful sexual relationships or producing and rearing healthy children. Under these circumstances, they may be married off to older already married or men in poor health. In short, women with disabilities do not have the same options of marriage and motherhood as non-disabled women.

Women with disabilities face violations of their rights at every level. They are considered a financial burden and social liability by their families; they are denied opportunities to movement outside the home and access to education; they are viewed as asexual, helpless and dependant; their vulnerability to physical, sexual and emotional abuse is enormous; their aspirations for marriage and parenthood often denied; they grow up ensconced with the walls of home or special institutions isolated and neglected with no hope of a normal life.

Needs of elderly women with disabilities—many of whom may be widows—deserve special mention. The combination of physical/mental disability and widowhood raises the spectre of a very precarious existence. Being powerless, isolated and anonymous women with disabilities are extremely vulnerable to abuse and violence. In addition, care-giving involving activities of daily living like dressing, eating and other bodily activities renders the disabled woman more vulnerable to abuse both at home and in institutions. She will be less able to defend herself in a risky situation because she may not be able to run or scream for help. Then, persons with developmental disabilities may be too trusting of others and hence may be easier to trick, bribe or coerce. They may not understand differences between sexual and non-sexual tactile behaviour. Persons with speech and hearing difficulties may have limited communication skills to report abuse. Furthermore since disabled persons are often taught to be obedient, passive and control their behaviour, this will render them easy victims.

Although a rights-based approach has entered the disability rights movement, the specific concerns of women with disabilities have found a place neither in the government policies and programmes nor the voluntary sector. Ironically or expectedly, the disabled rights movement all over the world including India is male dominated. It may even be blatantly sexist. Even within the women's movement, women with disabilities rarely figure as a distinct group.

2.2 Disaster-affected Women

Experiences have shown that effects of disasters (floods, droughts, riots) are profoundly discriminatory. Wherever they hit, pre-existing structures and social conditions determine that some members of the community pay a higher price. Among the differences that determine how people are affected by such disasters is that of gender. Lower status of women in general results in various kinds of exclusions and vulnerabilities in a disaster setting. Low mobility and lower access to information implies that women are often the last to receive relief resources. Women are disproportionately represented within the informal and agricultural sectors, which are the most adversely affected by disasters. This adversely affects their claim to relief and rehabilitation.

Thus, women experience high rates of unemployment, further decreasing their bargaining power within households and communities. Unlike men, they are the primary household caretakers and thus are not able to migrate for work. All these factors involving structural biases and gender discrimination result in the compensation amounts awarded being directed invariably at men.

Furthermore, domestic violence against women sharply increases after disasters and women face additional kinds of physical and sexual violence in relief camps. Disasters in which men die or migrate or are injured, women are left to lead households and communities, with few marketable skills and opportunities and even more vulnerability to violence and extortion. Women take on the responsibility for both caring for families and meeting livelihoods while having the least access to information, resources and opportunities.

Disasters create the potential to engage in long-term rights and equity-based development through practical strategies for gender empowerment. Successfully incorporating women within disaster management is one way to increase women's social, political and economic status in general, and to minimize the currently disproportionate impact of disasters on women. Strengthening the marketable skills of women, promoting livelihood options, enhancing women's leadership in micro-planning, relief and disaster mitigation and increasing their role in local governance are some of the strategies for adoption.

Practically, women have immense knowledge of their local environments and information about how to mitigate risks that lead to disasters. This knowledge can be transformed into actionable expertise by involving women within disaster management. Furthermore, women are the most effective in mobilizing communities, networks and institutions to pool resources, respond to disaster and create safety mechanisms.

Women are also most knowledgeable about those living within their communities, in terms of identifying marginalized groups and community trends.

Thus, a gender perspective must be incorporated whenever disaster prevention, mitigation and recovery strategies are being developed and implemented.

2.3 Migrant Women

Internal short-term migration for work (which may be seasonal) is now a widespread feature of rural India and reflects the continuing crisis of inadequate livelihood opportunities in rural areas. Increasingly, women are moving for work, not only with husbands or male members of families, but even on their own or in groups in search of work. Since the consequences of such migration are highly gendered, policies generating greater and more prolonged job opportunities for men and women within particular rural areas must be considered.

The migrant labourers generally work at whatever they can find, mostly contract work or casual work. The condition of migrant workers away from their homes is often pitiable. They get paid very less. They do not have access to clean water, sanitation, healthcare, public distribution system and have to buy their essentials at open market prices. Their children travel around with them and do not get education.

Male out-migration, when the families are left behind, affects the work burden of the women in rural areas. Women have to put in extraordinary amount of time to eke out a living, working in the field for wages or for subsistence, in addition to fetching fuel and fodder. The absence of men adds to material and psychological insecurity, leading to pressures and negotiations with wider family. Women may have to cope with a number of problems which are exacerbated due to the uncertainty of the timing and magnitude of remittances on which the precarious household economy depends. This, in turn, pushes women and children from poor labouring households to participate in the labour market under adverse conditions. The impact of male migration can be especially adverse for girls who often have to bear additional domestic responsibilities and take care of younger siblings. The absence of male supervision further reduces their chances of acquiring education. Incidence of women-headed households may also increase and it is to be noted that female-headed households are generally poorer than male-headed households.

The wages of the migrant husbands are either too infrequent or insufficient for constant sustenance of the family left behind. In fact, it is the free and hard work of women in sustaining the domestic economy, which helps to keep a large number of men working in town and cities at extremely low wages. Mobility and migration of workers make them more vulnerable, as a result of separation from spouse and release of social sanctions leading to high-risk sexual practices and consequently may contract HIV, which in turn is carried to their spouses and to their children. Public policy with respect to migration should cover issues affecting households of migrant workers, who are left without adult caregivers. It should also cover issues of protection and basic needs of migrant workers at their destination. Since women migrant workers face much greater threats to security and possibilities of violence, special measures should address this problem.

2.4 Women in Border Trade Areas

Women are the most vulnerable section of society in border trade centres and areas—which are adjacent to international borders and normally a *no-man's land*—controlled by anti-social elements and organizations that are inimical to the interests of the country. Under the circumstances, women, who are the major component in border trades, especially in agriculture and allied activities, are under severe threat. Matters are compounded by problems of infrastructure and facilities, which are either most rudimentary or simply do not exist. Access to health, education, drinking water, and sanitation is almost impossible, which adversely affect health.

Border trade centres/areas—besides normally being hot beds of smuggling, particularly of narcotics—are also centres of trafficking of women and children. Women are rendered vulnerable to all kinds of diseases, especially HIV/AIDS. Women are also used or forced into smuggling of narcotics, which makes them further vulnerable to law-enforcing agencies that are not sensitized to dealing with women law-breakers. The circle gets more vicious for women in these areas, many of whom are either illiterate or have received only rudimentary education and cannot be expected to be aware of their fundamental, human, legal and other rights. Problems of communication, organized marketing and non-implementation of labour laws also adversely affect women's economic power, which in turn reinforces them to play subservient roles and their empowerment continues to remain illusionary and elusive.

It is, therefore, necessary that some mechanism is set-up in border trade centres and areas to enforce the law of the land, as also to implement and monitor all fundamental, human, legal and other rights to ensure that no citizen of this country is denied and deprived of them.

Enhancing the utilization of the region's local and rich natural resources with appropriate technology for producing and marketing herbal products and processed food/fruits is another avenue to meet with the challenge posed by anti-social elements. Cold storages can be located in appropriate areas of the region, to sustain perishable items before they are transported to larger markets.

2.5 Women Left Behind due to Suicide by Farmer Husbands

Another highly vulnerable group are women who are left behind to take care of their children when their farmer husbands commit suicide on account of failure of crops or heavy indebtedness. These women face a whole host of problems—the possibility that they may not inherit the land holding; even if they did, they may not have the wherewithal to till the land as they do not have the necessary resources or access to credit, seeds, fertilizers etc.

The problem of inheriting debts which cannot be repaid may lead to distress sale of land without alternative livelihood options. The possibility of these women and their children being exploited or trafficked for nefarious purposes is very probable. There is an immediate need to develop a special package for women whose farmer husbands have committed suicide. The package should contain a comprehensive input of programmes of various sectors like agriculture, rural development, rural industries along with adequate support from micro credit facilities.

2.6 Other Vulnerable Groups of Women

2.6.1 Women Affected by Internal Displacements: There are problems associated with displacement caused by the introduction of huge development projects—like dams and special economic zones (SEZs)—in tribal and rural areas. Women have taken part in many of the agitations surrounding these projects. The loss of livelihoods has led to tribal women's increasing dependence on migration. Their work load has increased with the loss of traditional rights. They are also subjected to sexual violence, exploitation and trafficking. They are in conflict with many powers and interests, ranging from the state agencies to builders and landlords.

2.6.2 Adolescent Girls: Adolescent girls are one of the most vulnerable sections of society as they are subject to a number of problems:

1. Discrimination in terms of nutrition and food (malnutrition and anaemia rates for adolescents are quite significant).
2. School drop out.
3. Forced into sibling care.
4. Households work or even farm labour.
5. Domestic labour.
6. Trafficked for sexual exploitation.

7. Subjected to child marriages.
8. Frequent child bearing etc.

This is also the period during which girls can be truly empowered to make life-changing decisions and chart the course of their life in a most productive way. At present the programmatic interventions for adolescent girls are limited and sporadic and do not address the needs and requirements as an integrated whole. It is necessary to draw up a special package for their development which will take into account inter sectoral inputs.

2.6.3 Violence-affected Women:

1. Women who are victims of domestic violence.
2. Rape victims.
3. Trafficked-victim women.
4. Women who are labelled as witches.
5. Women who are victims of acid attacks.

2.6.4 Women as Labourers:

1. Women who work as domestic help.
2. Women who are bonded labour.
3. Destitute women who are homeless.

2.6.5 Women in Agriculture:

1. Landless women.
2. Marginal women farmers.
3. Women who work as agricultural workers.

2.6.6 Women from Minority Community: The main issues of Muslim minority women stem from three major factors: (a) insecurity, (b) exclusion and (c) poverty.

2.6.7 Single Women:

1. Adolescents.
2. Widows.
3. Women whose husbands are absent due to conflict, economic migration etc.
4. Divorcees.

2.6.8 Others

1. Women in Border Trade Areas.
2. Slum dwellers.

3. Women prisoners.
4. Women belonging to ethnic and religious minorities (especially Muslims).

3

Violence against Women

Gender discrimination and all other forms of discrimination—in particular racism, racial discrimination, xenophobia and related intolerance—continue to cause threat to the enjoyment of women of their human rights and fundamental freedoms. In situations of armed conflict and foreign occupation, human rights of women have been extensively violated.

In many countries, women have insufficient access to the law, resulting from illiteracy, lack of legal literacy, information and resources, insensitivity and gender bias, and lack of awareness of the human rights of women by law enforcement officials and the judiciary who in many cases fail to respect the human rights of women and the dignity and worth of the human person. There is insufficient recognition of women's and girls' reproductive rights, as well as barriers to their full enjoyment of those rights. Some women and girls continue to encounter barriers to justice and enjoyment of their human rights because of such factors as their race, language, ethnicity, culture, religion, disability or socio-economic class or because they are migrants, displaced women or refugees.

3.1 Human Rights in India

After Independence in 1947, legal reforms have been undertaken in India to prohibit all forms of discrimination and discriminatory provisions have been eliminated in civil, penal and personal status law governing marriage and family relations, women's property and ownership rights and work and employment rights. Steps have been taken to realize women's enjoyment of their human rights through the creation of an enabling environment, including the adoption of policy measures, the improvement of enforcement and monitoring mechanisms and the implementation of legal literacy and awareness campaigns at all levels.

The Constitution of India prohibits discrimination between men and women on the grounds of religion, sex, caste or place of birth, and enables the State to allow affirmative discrimination in favour of women as a fundamental right. By this principle, human rights as fundamental rights have been put on an equal footing for all. India has ratified significant international human rights instruments, including the ratification of the Convention on Elimination of All Forms of Discrimination against Women (CEDAW), 1993.

Government has created independent national institutions for the protection and promotion of human rights of all citizens, especially women, religious minorities and caste-based communities.

1. National Human Rights Commission (NHRC), 1994.
2. National Commission for Minorities, 1992.
3. National Commission for Scheduled Castes and Scheduled Tribes, 1990.
4. National Commission for Women, 1990.

28 States Governments and Union Territories have set up State Commissions for Women to act as statutory ombudspersons. Human Rights Commissions have been set up in 9 states.

The Supreme Court of India through its activist role has infused dynamism into the constitutional and legal provisions and has issued directives to the State from time to time to further safeguard and strengthen the rights of women. Through a series of public interest litigation (PIL), any person/persons who in the event of violation of rights and is unable to approach the Court (by reason of poverty, disability, social or economic advantage) can maintain an application for an appropriate direction, order or writ. This has further contributed to the cause of gender justice. Certain landmark judgements of the Supreme Court on matters such as the need for a Uniform Civil Code for all women irrespective of religion, the need for equal property rights for women, particularly in the case of inheritance, pronouncements on child prostitution, need for in-camera trial of rape victims etc. are evidence of an activist role of the Court.

To effectively deal with the problem cf violence against women, and to bridge the gap between public and the private sphere, there have been numerous governmental and non-governmental interventions. The government is working in two steps. In the first step, it is working towards the strengthening of the existing legislation through review and amendments, wherever required, and developing institutional mechanisms, i.e. National and State Commissions for Women, women police cells in police stations and *all-women police stations*, etc. Its other course of action centres around running projects that provide support to vulnerable women, rehabilitation of victims of violence through schemes like *Swadhar*, and setting up of help lines for women in distress. Family courts have been set up in some States to adjudicate cases relating to maintenance, custody and divorce.

3.2 Forms of Violence against Women

Violence against women (VAW) includes any act of gender-based violence that results in, or is likely to result in, physical, sexual or psychological harm or suffering to women, including threats of such acts, coercion or arbitrary deprivation of liberty, whether occurring in public or private life. Violence against women manifests itself in many ways and is one of the most pervasive forms of human rights abuse in the world today. While all women may experience violence, it intersects with other social and identity-based constructs like caste, religion, ethnicity, disability, and sexual orientation to make specific groups vulnerable to different and particular forms of violence. Thus, the nature of the violence and how it manifests itself may differ because of social location.

Forms of violence that take place at the community level include witch hunting, sati, child marriage, and incidents of public stripping. These unfortunately are increasing in prevalence. In recent years there have been disturbing reports of cases of sati and its subsequent glorification. There has been an alarming rise in reported cases of honour crimes committed in the name of protecting family or community honour. Equally worrying is the growing numbers of anti-women strictures being pronounced by community-based structures like caste and religious panchayats. The brunt of these so-called judgments—which in some cases have resulted in brutal punishments such as dismemberment and mutilation—are usually borne by women or the women's family.

Many such actions follow when women try and change age-old, narrow and regressive social norms like marrying outside one's caste or religion. Many of these so-called judgments are not only anti-women but go against the Constitution.

Experiences from the ground and various reports are now showing that women are specifically targeted in situations of communal and sectarian violence as they embody the so-called honour of the community. If a particular community or group is to be attacked and humiliated, women are targeted. In such situations women are victims of various forms of sexual violence including rape, molestation, mutilation, stripping etc.

Yet another form of violence relates to *acid attacks* on women. This is a heinous form of violence against women and has lasting impact on their autonomy and freedom of movement.

It is widely accepted that violence against women and girls, whether occurring in public or private life, is a human rights issue. It is also accepted that states have an obligation to exercise due diligence to prevent investigate and punish acts of violence whether those acts are perpetrated by the state or private persons and provide protection to victims. There is increased awareness and commitment to prevent and combat violence against women and girls, including domestic violence, which violates, impairs and nullifies the enjoyment of their human rights and fundamental freedoms.

Women continue to be victims of various forms of

violence. Inadequate understanding of the root causes of all forms of violence against women and girls hinders efforts to eliminate violence against women and girls. Inadequate data on violence further impede informed policymaking and analysis. Socio-cultural attitudes which are discriminatory and economic inequalities reinforce women's subordinate place in society. This makes women and girls vulnerable to many forms of violence—physical, sexual and psychological—occurring in the family. This may include battering, sexual abuse of female children in the household, dowry-related violence, marital rape, female genital mutilation and other traditional practices harmful to women.

Domestic violence—including sexual violence in marriage—is still treated as a private matter in some countries. Insufficient awareness of the consequences of domestic violence, how to prevent it, and the rights of victims still exists. Although improving, the legal and legislative measures—especially in the criminal justice area to eliminate different forms of violence against women and children, including domestic violence and child pornography—are weak in many countries. It is also noted that in some countries problems have arisen from the use of new information and communication technologies for trafficking in women and children and for the purposes of all forms of economic and sexual exploitation.

Violence against women and girls is a major obstacle to the achievement of the objectives of gender equality, development and peace. Main forms of gender-based violence include the following:

1. Battering and other domestic violence.
2. Sexual abuse.
3. Sexual slavery and exploitation.
4. Trafficking in women and children.
5. Forced prostitution and sexual harassment.

The main reasons for gender-based violence are the following:

1. Cultural prejudice.

2. Racism and racial discrimination.
3. Xenophobia.
4. Pornography.
5. Ethnic cleansing.
6. Armed conflict.
7. Foreign occupation.
8. Religious and anti-religious extremism.
9. Terrorism.

Violence against women is incompatible with the dignity and worth of the human person and must be combated and eliminated.

3.3 Sexual Harassment of Women

The National Commission for Women (NCW) prepared a code of conduct for the work place and circulated the same to all ministries, educational institutions, public and private sector undertakings and various NGOs for information and implementation.

The University Grants Commission has formulated a code of conduct for students and staff of Universities. The Central Board of Secondary Education (CBSE) has taken action to ensure that all affiliated schools and educational institutions abide by these guidelines. All Ministries have set up complaint committees to look into such matters.

In a case of sexual harassment of a woman at the workplace, the inquiry conducted by the complaints committee should be deemed as inquiry conducted in a departmental inquiry under the disciplinary proceedings, drawn up against the delinquent official. The Department of Personnel and Training has informed all Ministries/Departments of Government of India that the findings of the complaints committee regarding sexual harassment of the complainant/victim will be binding on the disciplinary authority to initiate disciplinary proceedings against the government servant(s). The report of the complaints committee should be treated as the preliminary report against the accused government servant.

3.4 Rape and Sexual abuse

The increased incidence of rape cases in recent times may be because more cases are being reported now. Currently, the crime of rape is dealt with in Sections 375-377 of the Indian Penal Code.

The Supreme Court in Delhi Domestic Working Women's Forum vs. Union of India and others writ petition (CRL) No. 362/93 had directed the National Commission for Women to evolve a "scheme so as to wipe out the tears of unfortunate victims of rape". It observed that given the Directive principles contained in Article 38(1) of the Constitution, it was necessary to set up a Criminal Injuries Compensation Board. Besides the mental anguish, rape victims frequently incur substantial financial loss and in some cases are too traumatized to continue in employment. The Court further directed that compensation for victims shall be awarded by the Court on conviction of the offender and by the Criminal Injuries Compensation Board irrespective of whether or not a conviction has taken place. The Board shall take into account pain, suffering and shock as well as loss of earnings due to pregnancy and the expenses of child birth if this occurs as a result of rape. Accordingly, NCW has drafted a scheme titled "Relief and Rehabilitation of Rape Victims".

The Supreme Court of India has ruled that delay by rape victims in filing complaints against the accused cannot be used as a defence to escape conviction. A division bench of the Supreme Court ruled in September 2004 that lower courts could not "disregard" the prosecution case because a first information report (FIR) had been filed late.

In addition to the above, other gender-specific crimes that have been recognized under the IPC and special laws are *sati*, bigamy, molestation, obscenity, indecent representation of women, kidnapping, abduction and importation of girls. Aspects of investigation, arrest and prosecution of these crimes are the responsibility of state governments. The criminal justice system has to pay particular attention to the needs of women who are subjected to these specific forms of violence.

3.5 Trafficking in Women

Human trafficking, both forced and under false promises, is widespread, but no accurate data is available. Trafficking, however, is usually and wrongly, conflated with prostitution. The purposes of trafficking include, (besides prostitution), entertainment, industry, forced labour, domestic work, camel jockeys, illegal adoption of children, bonded labour, forced marriage, drug trafficking, begging etc.

Poverty, breakdown in livelihood options, food insecurity, unemployment, debts, occurrence of disasters, and conflicts leave the victims, particularly women, in miserable situations with practically no choices for survival. Girls are also trafficked in the name of marriage. Victims often find themselves unwillingly trapped in a life of physical and sexual abuse.

The situation of women who have been trafficked into sex work is particularly vulnerable. They have little control over their earnings and face the risk of pregnancies, abortions, maternal mortality, sexually transmitted diseases such as HIV and AIDS. The Immoral Trafficking (Prevention) Act, 1956 penalizes all persons involved in trafficking women for sex work and living off their income. Unfortunately, the law has been implemented in a highly moralistic manner resulting in the further victimization of trafficked women. The objective of the Act, i.e. the punishment of those involved in trafficking has not been met.

The problem of cross border trafficking especially of young children and women from Bangladesh and Nepal into India, has been growing in recent years. Central Sector Scheme called *Ujjawala* was launched on December 4, 2007. The scheme consists of five components:

1. **Prevention:** Formation of community vigilance groups and adolescent groups. Awareness and sensitisation of functionaries like police, community leaders though preparation of IEC material and workshops.
2. **Rescue:** Safe withdrawal of the victim from the place of exploitation.

3. **Rehabilitation:** Provision of safe shelter for victims with fulfilment of basic needs such food, clothing, counselling, medical care, legal aid, and vocational training and income generation activities.
4. **Reintegration:** Restoration of the victim to the family/community (only if she desires) and covering costs of the same.
5. **Repatriation:** Support to cross-border victims for their safe repatriation to the country of their origin.

3.6 Sexual Harassment of Women at Workplace

In India, women are entering the labour workforce in unprecedented numbers. In the light of this development, there is, more than ever before, a pressing need for the rights of women to be respected and protected, particularly at the workplace. Further, with the greater representation of women in the unorganized sector, there is a need for institutions and a policy to be set up to empower women.

Women's rights at the workplace are important for many reasons. The obvious reason is the right of women to be free from unwanted sexual conduct and advances. The issue of sexual harassment at the workplace extends far beyond an individual woman. It impacts on workforce productivity, economic development, and the overall growth of the country.

The Supreme Court in the case of *Vishaka vs. State of Rajasthan* held that sexual harassment at the workplace is a violation of the rights guaranteed by Articles 14, 15 and 21 and that women have rights to gender equality, to work with dignity in a safe working environment and be protected from sexual harassment or abuse. The court in this case defined "*sexual harassment at the workplace*" and issued a set of guidelines for employers to redress and prevent this kind of violation of women's human rights at workplace.

Since then, various government establishments have amended their respective statutes for the prevention and addressing complaints of sexual harassment. However, a large section of women in the private and the unorganized sector are still unprotected.

4

Declining Child Sex Ratio in India

In 1996, the World Health Assembly endorsed the fact that violence against women is a public health problem and female foeticide is one extreme manifestation of violence against women. This can be one of the most glaring examples of violation of human rights and striking at the roots of the concept of dignity of women or elimination of discrimination. [1] With the technological advances, the latest scientific techniques are used to abort female foetuses. With sufficient availability and extensive supply of such sophisticated sex determination techniques in the health institutions and clinics, there have been hundreds of incidences of female foeticide surfacing and hence assuming an alarming proportion across the country at present.

4.1 India's Demographic Characteristics

After China, India is the most populated country in the world with a headcount of 121 crore in 2011. Mainland China's population is 135 crore.

4.1.1 Importance of Census: The Indian Census—a decadal exercise—is the most credible source of information on demography (population characteristics), economic activity, literacy and education, housing and household amenities, urbanisation, fertility and mortality, scheduled castes and scheduled tribes, language, religion, migration, disability and many other socio-cultural and demographic data. Census 2011 was the 15th headcount of India's population since 1872. This is the only source of primary data in the village, town and ward level. It provides valuable information for planning and formulation of policies for Central and the State Governments and is widely used by national and international Agencies, scholars, business people, industrialists, and many more.

Delimitation/reservation of constituencies—parliamentary, assembly, panchayats and other local bodies—is also done on the basis of the demographic data collected by the Census. Census is the basis for reviewing the country's progress in the past decade, monitoring the on-going schemes of the Government and most importantly, plan for the future.

4.1.2 Population Growth: India's population has increased rapidly since Independence in 1947. The population increased from 36.1 crore in 1951 to 43.9 crore in 1961, to 54.8 crore in 1971, and to 68.5 crore in 1981. The census of 1991 enumerated the population at 84.4 crore which rose to 102.9 crore in 2001 and was estimated at 121 crore in 2011. Thus, after China it is India that has crossed the 1 billion (100 crore) population mark. According to a recent United Nations publication, India's population is projected to peak at 1.718 billion (171 crore) in 2060. At its peak, India will be the most populous country in the world. China at its peak in 2025 will have 1.395 billion (139.5 crore) people. In fact, when China peaks, India will have already surpassed it in population. [2]

Population of India increased from 103 crore in 2001 to 121 crore in 2011, an increase of 18 crore or 17.6 percent. Out of 121 crore, 62.4 crore were males and 58.6 crore were females.

More precisely, India added 18.1 crore people to its population between 2001 and 2011 against 18.2 crore in the preceding decade. However, even 18.1 crore equals the total population of Brazil, the world's fifth most populous country.

For the first time since Independence in 1947, India added fewer people to its population in the decade just ended (2001-2011) than in the previous one. While decadal population growth rates have consistently been declining since the 1960s, the absolute addition in each decade was always higher than in the previous decade. That is now changed.

At 121 crore, India's population is almost equal to the combined population of US, Indonesia, Brazil, Pakistan, Bangladesh and Japan. Mainland China's population is 135 crore.

Uttar Pradesh remains the most populous state (19.95 crore) followed by Maharashtra (11.2 crore) in 2011. These 2 states put together surpass US, the world's third most populous country after China and India, in population.

The unabated growth of population is attributable to a sharp decline in death-rate coupled with relatively high birth-rate. The death-rate (7.1 per thousand in 2011) has fallen due to improved health conditions, control of epidemics, better handling of famine conditions, and general improvement in the standard of living. There has been a significant decline in the infant mortality rate since Independence.

However, birth-rate in India is still very high (21.8 per thousand in 2011). Many social and economic factors are responsible for high birth-rate. These include universality of marriage, preference for male children, illiteracy, and poverty. The rapid growth of population has seriously hampered developmental efforts.

The projections of population made by National Commission for Enterprises in the Unorganized Sector (NCEUS) in its report titled *The Challenge of Employment in India: An Informal Economy Perspective* (April 2009) are presented in Table 1.1

Table 1.1: Projected Population and Growth Rates in Different Years by Sex

(million)

Year	Male	Female	Total
2002	541.68	505.30	1046.98
2007	584.78 (1.54)	545.19 (1.53)	1129.97 (1.54)
2012	626.63 (1.39)	583.70 (1.37)	1210.32 (1.38)
2017	665.48 (1.21)	619.41 (1.19)	1284.89 (1.20)

Source: National Commission for Enterprises in the Unorganized Sector (NCEUS), *The Challenge of Employment in India: An Informal Economy Perspective*, April 2009, Volume I, Table 5.1, p. 104.

4.1.3 Overall Sex Ratio: The census also records overall sex ratio, which is the number of females to every 1,000 males across all ages. In 1921, the number of females per thousand males was 955. There were many reasons for excess of male over female population. The lack of pre-natal and post-natal care was the major cause of high death-rate among women in reproductive age. The evil practice of female infanticide in some parts of the country during British rule also contributed to reduced share of female population in total population.

Even during the post-Independence period, the trend of sex ratio in India has been in favour of masculine population. According to the 1991 census, there were 927 females per thousand males. As per 2001 Census, the sex ratio stood at 933 females per 1,000 males, a marginal improvement over 1991. The persistent tendency towards low sex ratio can be attributed to lack of attention and care given to female children, sex selective female abortions, and the higher death-rate among women in the reproductive age. It is noteworthy that in Western countries, the sex ratio favours the feminine population.

Improved medical technology, education and improvement in quality of life during the first decade of the 21st century resulted in the overall gender ratio improving from 933 in 2001 to 940 in 2011. This is in line with general improvement in the overall sex ratio since 1991. Only 3 major states showed a decline in their sex ratio: J&K, Bihar and Gujarat.

Delhi and Haryana are the states with the worst overall sex ratios (866 and 877 respectively). In fact, a healthy sex ratio remains largely a southern phenomenon. Kerala is the only state where women outnumber men (1,084 females for every 1,000 males). Next in order is Tamil Nadu with 995 females for every 1,000 males.

4.1.4 Child Sex Ratio (0-6 years): The data show that the sex ratio for children below 6 years (i.e. number of girls for every 1,000 boys) dropped from 927 in 2001 to a dismal 914 in 2011 (Table 1.2). This decline is unabated since 1961 Census. Among big states, Chhattisgarh has the highest child sex ratio of 964 followed by Kerala with 959. Haryana is at the bottom (830) followed by Punjab (846). This gender bias draws attention to a lingering societal flaw which economic growth is not being able to correct.

Table 1.2: Recent Trends in Sex Ratio and Child Sex Ratio (0-6 years) in India

Year	Sex Ratio	Child Sex Ratio
1991	927	945
2001	933	927
2011	940	914

Source: Census of India, 2011.

As a result of this declining sex ratio, millions of girls/women are missing in India. It is an alarming scenario and if this trend continues, violence against women would increase and there would be forced polyandry. The demographic balance would be permanently damaged.

One of the reasons for the declining sex ratios is the incidence of sex selection, and or sex determination followed by sex selective abortions. This constitutes a grave form of discrimination against women as women are affected as being part of a social class. This is not a pro-life or pro-choice issue. A woman's right to abortion has to be upheld on grounds of promoting women's rights to equality. The right to abortion is the right to abort any foetus. The abortion of a female foetus following a sex determination test is an act of discrimination. As this act of discrimination cannot be committed without the active intervention of medical professionals, it is essential to strictly enforce laws directed towards regulating the practice of medical professionals. However, keeping in mind the pressures that a woman is subjected to for bearing a male child, the implementation and enforcement of such laws should not lead to the further victimization of women.

The laws regulating sex determination and abortions are provided for in the Pre-conception and Pre-natal Diagnostic Techniques (Prohibition of Misuse) Act and the Medical

Termination of Pregnancies Act 1971. In addition, penal provisions on "causing miscarriages" are also provided in Sections 312-316 of the Indian Penal Code.

Sex determination before birth is widely prevalent. Certain districts in Punjab and Haryana account for a substantial drop in the decennial child sex ratio. Richer districts tend to account for a larger decline in the child sex ratio. The incidence of the use of sex determination techniques tends to be more in the most modern and developed districts. This calls into question the argument that the market economy undermines patriarchal authoritarian and male-biased traditional attitudes and spreads egalitarian values. Policy has to address the concern that inculcation of the values of market economy seems to be only enhancing gender inequity as reflected in the female foeticide and infanticide indicators.

There are two important issues of policy associated with this decline in the child sex ratio. One is the obsession with population control, which assumes that all the failures in development can be mono-causally linked to population explosion. The other more recent issue is the intrusion of the two-child norm into the Panchayati Raj Acts of many states, despite its absence from the Population Policy of 2000, leading to disqualification of many elected representatives. Most of the excluded belong to the scheduled castes (SCs) and scheduled tribes (STs). Some experts have suggested a link between the imposition of the two-child norm and sex selective abortions. Imposition of the two-child norm, then, cannot be the route to population stabilisation, for it may lead to a disturbingly unbalanced population.

Ironically, the deficit of woman is more noticeable in the urban than the rural population—a factor which is frequently attributed to male migration from rural to urban areas. The deficit has now percolated down to the rural areas as well indicating an overall decrease of woman in the country. The district analysis of the child sex ratio in rural areas calculated from the 1991 census shows that there are only 42 districts, making up 10 percent of the country, where the sex ratio is in favour of girls. Of these, 31 districts like 2 in Tamil Nadu, 1 in Kerala, and 11 out of 12 in Punjab, where there are less than 900 girls to 1,000 boys.

4.2 Status of Women in Indian Society

The status of women in India has been a chequered one as it has seen many ups and downs. In the Vedic Age 1500-1000 B.C., they were worshipped as goddesses. In the Muslim age 1026-1756 A.D. their status suffered a sharp decline and in the British regime they were looked down upon as 'slaves of slaves'. [3] Punjab has a long history of doing away with new born girls. The preferred method today is foeticide after a sex determination test, but centuries ago the practice was to bury them. This tradition perhaps goes back to the days of repeated invasions by Muslim armies from the northwest, who used to carry off girls as booty for their own pleasure or to be sold in the slave markets of the Middle East. Today, it is the extortionate dowries that parents of girls have to provide upon marriage. The custom of polyandry in Punjab probably arose out of the shortage of girls—the eldest son of a family would take a wife, his younger brothers would also have access to her.

Studies report that women in southern India enjoy a better status irrespective of their literacy in comparison to their north Indian counterparts. [4] It has long been argued that improvement in literacy rates and socioeconomic development amongst women could change the adverse sex ratio for the better. However, it has been observed that educated mothers in Punjab are more prone to discriminate against their daughters than the uneducated ones. Also, the prevalence of prenatal sex determination is more widespread among the economically well-off because availing of such services is determined by one's ability to pay. Thus, the rich agriculturists living in the rural areas of Punjab, Haryana and Gujarat and the urban elite living in the Metropolis of Delhi tend to avail of sex selective abortion. [5]

After Independence, and the passing of the Hindu Code Bill giving equal rights to inherit ancestral property to sons and daughters, things again took a turn for the worse with the murder of new-born girls gaining momentum, especially in propertied families. With medical science able to detect the sex of the child in the womb, the practice has become much more widespread, resulting in a situation today where the ratio of females to males in Punjab is the lowest in the country.

When daughters are born, families must hold back on economic resources to save for gifts to the woman's future husband and his family. For example, girls are denied the right to education, since expenses on their education is not considered to be an investment of higher returns. According to Janice Raymond, girls are breastfed for a shorter period of time, which denies their right to adequate health and nutrition. Girls are also not immunized, failure of which leads to poor health and sickness. There is suggestion that this can be a deliberate attempt to limit their lives. [6] Women in India have made some progress in the fields of education, health or economics or as a result of technological development, or because of a process of evolution.

Though in small number, the representation of women can be seen in all walks of the life. Women of today are doctors, engineers, pilots, journalists, administrators, judges including woman Judges in the Supreme Court, state governors, ambassadors, Member of Parliament and ministers. India has had a woman Prime Minister and a President of the UN Assembly. In spite of these achievements the fact remains that ordinary women's condition is a grim reality. According to the 1981 census report there were 933 women per 1,000 men, and 47 percent literate men compared with 25 percent of women who were literate. Dowry deaths, child marriages, the perpetuation of widowhood and the preference for a son continue to have social sanctions. As for the child marriages, out of the total of 321 million females, 147 million or 47 percent were married and of these 2.63 million or 1.79 percent were in the age group of 10-14 years. In the rural areas, out of 115 million married females, 2.42 million or 2.41 percent were aged between 10-14 years. In the urban areas the figures are relatively smaller, out of 32.14 million, 0.68 percent in the age group of 10-14 years. [7]

4.3 Gender Bias System

Gender bias is a preference or prejudice toward one gender over the other. Bias can be conscious or unconscious, and may manifest in many ways, both subtle and obvious. In many countries, eliminating gender bias is the basis of many laws, including those that govern workplaces, family courts, and even the voting booth. Despite these efforts, many legal and political scholars argue that total gender parity remains a far off goal, one which many regions are not remotely close to reaching.

Some of the worst gender ratios, indicating gross violation of women's rights, are found in South and East Asian countries such as India and China. The determination of the sex of the foetus by ultrasound scanning, amniocentesis, and in vitro fertilization has aggravated this situation. No moral or ethical principle supports such a procedure for gender identification. The situation is further worsened by a lack of awareness of women's rights and by the indifferent attitude of governments and medical professionals. In India, the available legislation for prevention of sex determination needs strict implementation, alongside the launching of programmes aimed at altering attitudes, including those prevalent in the medical profession.

The bias against females in India is grounded in cultural, economic and religious roots. Sons are expected to work in the fields, provide greater income and look after parents in old age. In this way, sons are looked upon as a type of insurance. Says Senthil, a labourer at a housing construction site, who has a daughter and son, "When our son was born, we were very happy. After all, in the long-run, he is the one who is going to provide us his income and take care of us in our old age.

Also, as per Hindu belief, lighting the funeral pyre by a son is considered necessary for salvation of the spirit. [8] This strong preference for sons which results in a life endangering deprivation of daughters is not considered abhorrent culturally and socially. [9]

Even our religions have been prejudiced towards women. According to Manu (2000 B.C.-2000 A.D.), a woman has to be reborn as a man to attain moksha (redemption). A man cannot attain *moksha* unless he has a son to light his pyre. A male offspring alone guarantees moksha. And he attains eternity through a grandson. Also, it says a woman who gives birth to only daughters may be left in the eleventh year of marriage.

Family lineage and the family name are carried on by male children in many societies, leading parents concerned about their family's future generations to hope for a son and possibly murder or abort girl children in order to get an heir. Some societies practice rigid social customs that make girls much more expensive to raise than boys.

Traditional cultural practices reflect deeply rooted values and benefits. Son preference is exhibited in many cultures and is not unique to developing countries or rural areas, although it is stronger in countries where patriarchy and partiality are prevalent. Societies that expect women to live and express themselves within narrowly defined gender roles also often exhibit cultural practices that benefit man and harm women and girl children.

Such gender bias leads to incidences such as female foeticide and female infanticide. According to Malavika Karlekar, editor, Indian Journal of Gender Studies, "Those women who undergo sex determination tests and abort on knowing that the foetus is female are actively taking a decision against equality and the right to life for girls. In many cases, of course, the women are not independent agents but merely victims of a dominant family ideology based on preference for male children".

4.4 Women and Social Structure

'Women as a class are half the mankind'. The Commission on the Status of Women under the U.N. plays a constructive role in raising women to the dignity of a free human-being and to guide the General Assembly of the U.N. in preventing any discrimination against women in any part of the world.

The present education system both for men and women does not prepare better individuals who can become forward looking citizens. The education we have is an education for *status quo*; it is not tailored to instigate rapid social change and development. It does not prepare a person to ask, to question, to be intellectually bold and honest. All that the students are taught to do is to receive instruction and digest facts and figures.

Women are glorified for being the preservers of culture anti of tradition. This very often means that women are more tradition bound and less progressive. The modernity of educated girls and women should not remain "dress deep" which is very often the case". It is often observed that in matters of dressing up, make up etc., they incur the wrath of their parents; they become the butt of criticism. But in those matters where they should really be changing and revolting them very obediently follow the advice of their parents. For example, it is seldom that one finds educated women revolting against the curse of dowry, rebelling against arranged marriages, opposing the wasteful expenditure on enormous feasts and decorations at weddings.

The biological and social sciences no longer admit the existence of unchanged fixed entities that determine characteristics such as those ascribed to women. All our socialisation is based on sexual lines. Certain temperamental characteristics are expected from women and so also certain stages of life and gesture. Right from the childhood, the young girls are given different toys to play, different dresses to wear and different manners to be imbibed. The distinctions revealed through the assumption of roles on the basis of sex are purely cultural without any biological or any other basis which could locate these differences in the inmate or inherent nature of men and women. These cultural differences are institutionalised in the social system. The individuals in the social system accept and adopt their life styles and consider them natural for their sexes, like various customs and traditions which we accept without question. [10]

The tasks of cooking and looking after children are not biological, men also can do. The present set up is advantageous to men. Women can take up any modern job which men can with same ease and efficiency. But in modern society, the occupational role of women is merely an extension of her sexual sides. The sectors of employment open to her are often an extension of the female role. A young and pretty woman can be an air hostess and no one is surprised at seeing her travel to far corners of the earth. Should she want to be a pilot, an international lawyer, a reporter etc., she would be barred in practice, if not in law. World travel is authorized for a woman if she is making use of her beauty, but if she uses her intelligence, it is prohibited. Intelligence is distributed among men and women as an instinct of nature, not on sex. If women were given some opportunities like men, the progress of the world would have been manifold.

4.5 Female Foeticide Defined

Killing of female child has been a phenomenal characteristic of Indian society under the rule of patriarchy since ancient days. The survey of the crimes scene revealed that both, young girls and older women are denied a decent living in our country; it is only the next step in this cruel logic that they should be denied life itself. Female infanticide, snuffling out the lives of new-born babies, and female foeticide is the ultimate catharsis in the tragic drama of female life in this country. [11]

The Indian Penal Code takes care of the child from its foetal stage. Miscarriage is punished in law because it involves the performance of an operation dangerous to life of the mother and because it arrests the growth of population which is essential for the existence and welfare of society. At the same time, circumstances arise when performance of the operation alone can save the life of the mother. In that case its performance becomes justifiable and the law then allows the sacrifice of one rudimentary life to save another comparatively more valuable. [12]

Female foeticide or sex selective abortion is the elimination of the female foetus in the womb itself. The sex of the foetus is determined by methods like amniocentesis, [13] Chiron villous biopsy [14] and now by the most popular technique ultrasonography. [15] Once the sex of the foetus is determined, if it is a female foetus, it is aborted. The increase in female foeticide has seen proportionate decrease in female sex ratio which has hit an all-time low especially in the 0-6 age group and if this decline is not checked the very delicate equilibrium of nature can be permanently destroyed.

It is also defined as aborting a female foetus after sex determination test or pre-natal diagnostic test which includes the following: (a) ultra-solography, (b) foetoscopy, (c) placental tissue sampling and (d) amniocentesis. [16]

The practice first dubbed as female infanticide came into vogue due to the lack of scientific discovery and unavailability of modern and progressive technology and sophisticated sex determining instruments. With sufficient availability and extensive supply of sophisticated sex determination techniques in the health institutions and clinics, there have been hundreds of incidences of female foeticide surfacing and hence assuming an alarming proportion across the country at present. It seems that the sex determination test leading to identification of the sex of unborn child has made the practice of killing the female child easier than before. The practice that commenced in India under the influence of the deeply rooted patriarchy, that is, to prove the strength of man over woman, has also been influenced by poverty and dowry.

4.6 Incidence and Magnitude of Female Foeticide

Sex selective abortions cases have become a significant social phenomenon in several parts of India. It transcends all castes, class and communities and even the North South dichotomy. The girl children become target of attack even before they are born. Diaz, states that in a well-known Abortion Centre in Mumbai, after undertaking the sex determination tests, out of the 15,914 abortions performed during 1984-85 almost 100 percent were those of girl foetuses. Similarly, a survey report of women's centre in Mumbai found that out of 8,000 foetuses aborted in six city hospitals 7,999 foetuses were of girls. It is reported that about 4,000 female babies are aborted in Tamil Nadu (southern India) every year. Sex determination tests are widely resorted to even in the remotest rural areas. Since most deliveries in rural areas take place at home, there is no record of the exact number of births/deaths that take place.

Therefore, it is difficult to assess the magnitude of the problem. However, the fact remains that the right to be born are being denied to the female child. Since all religions treated abortion as immoral, and contrary to divine law, this blanket ban on abortion, resulted in illegal abortions and risking the life of the woman. Though a series of government circulars banned the sex determination tests from 1977 onwards yet a field study conducted in Mumbai by Sanjeev Kulkarni (1986) brought to light the fact that 84 percent of the gynaecologists admitted to having performed the amniocentesis tests for sex determination. Of these, 74 percent gynaecologists had started performing the test since 1982 and only a few cases of genetic defects were detected.

The overwhelming majority of 'patients', most of whom were from middle or upper middle class, were only interested in knowing the sex of the foetus. Interestingly, it was found that 64 percent of the abortion service providers were against sex selective abortions; 10 percent said they were against it but had to do it and the rest about 24 percent approved the practice of sex selective abortions. Although there was not much variation among service providers working in public/private health care facilities or rural/urban location but difference was found among men and women service providers. About 28 percent men approved of sex selective abortion practice whereas it was only 17 percent in case of women providers. Thus, it was a higher percentage of women providers (68 percent) compared to men (61 percent) who were against such a practice. Those who disapproved of the practice of sex selective abortions but engaged in it against their principles expressed their compulsions and helplessness for two reasons:

1. Due to pressures arising out of unhealthy competition in the health care service sector it was said that if they did not provide abortion care services, some others would have provided them, and
2. Implications in terms of persistent abuse and exploitation that the women have to face back home in case they did not get the abortion done.

Many people have talked about the compulsions that women have to go for sex selection abortions. These arise either out of social norms fostering son preference or because their lives are put at stake in case they do not produce a son. Some also said that unwanted girls ran the risk of severe ill treatment at their natal homes causing them emotional and mental trauma. Hence, the service providers empathised with the woman's social needs for sex selective abortions. Nearly 10,000 cases of female foeticide have been reported from Ahmedabad alone. Additional threat that causes grave concern is the development of new pre-selection techniques, such as, electrophoresis, ericsson's method etc., which involve prior manipulation of the sex of the child. What will be the future of the female race is a moot question. There is dearth of empirical data on this subject. Sections 312-316 of the Indian Penal Code (IPC) deal with miscarriage and death of an unborn child and depending upon the severity and intention with which the crime is committed, the penalties range from seven years to life imprisonment for fourteen years and fine.

4.7 Female Foeticide and Infanticide

Another form of eliminating the girl child has been the practice of female infanticide. "Female infanticide is the intentional killing of baby girls due to the preference for male babies and from low value associated with the birth of females".

Kolloor (1990) defines infanticide as, "killing of an entirely dependent child under "one year of age" who is killed by mother, parents or others in whose care the child is entrusted". Infanticide is the secret burial of child weather dead or alive and is forbidden by the law. Section 318 is intended to prevent infanticide by penalising the disposal of corpus deliciti for the purpose of preventing its detection. Any concealment of birth by secret, disposal of the body with an intentional view to withhold the disclosure of the birth of the child from the world is punishable. The provision designedly serves the interest of the infant who otherwise cannot find himself in a position to protect him. Section 318 of Indian Penal Code, makes punishable, secret burial or otherwise disposal of the dead body of a child whether such child dies before or after or during its birth. For purposes of this section, it is enough to show that child was born and that the child was sufficiently developed to have lived, if born alive.

In *Sailbala Dasi vs. Emperor* [17], the birth took place in the medical school hospital and was attended by nurses and others in hospital who were aware that the accused had given birth to twins and it was known to two women when the nurse endeavoured to persuade to adopt the children and another relative of the woman (also accused) knew about the birth. It was held that there was no concealment of birth.

In a case (1 Nag, L.R., 89), a pregnant woman went to jungle to ease herself, there she gave birth to a child, who died immediately. Leaving the dead body there, the woman came back. It was held that mere leaving of the dead body, where the birth took place, did not constitute a secret burial. [18]

In *State vs. Kehari Singh Konsa* [19], a Rajput widow gave birth to an illegitimate child, who died soon after its birth. Kehari Singh, her uncle, took the dead body of the child and threw it in a well. Both of them were prosecuted under Section 318 of Indian Penal code, but were acquitted by the sessions court. In the appeal against acquittal, the High court held that from the prosecution evidence, it is evident that many villagers knew that Konsa was pregnant and that she gave birth to an illegitimate child. Therefore, the disposal of the dead body of that child was not with the intention of concealing the birth of the child. Hence, the appeal was dismissed. The law requires that the child should be dead at the time of its secret burial or disposal. If the child was living at the time and the girl merely consented at the instance of the father to the said child being delivered to a third person, the offence is not made out (1958 All. L.J. 707).

In *Lachhaman Kumar vs. State* [20], the appellant's pregnancy was known to all. Having given birth to an illegitimate child, she took it in her sari and witnesses saw one of its legs and she was prosecuted for having murdered it and disposed it off with a view to conceal its birth. She was acquitted of the charge of murder but was convicted under this section. In the appeal, the High court held that appellant might have contemplated a secret disposal of the body, but in as much as her intention was not given effect to it could not be held that offence was completed. Hence, she was acquitted.

Female foeticide means killing the female foetus in the mother's womb and the same offence can be committed with or without the consent of the woman. Section 312 relates to the causing of miscarriage with her consent while Section 313 deals with the same operation performed without her consent.

In *Manuddin Khan vs. State of M.P.* [21], the High Court held that if facts of pregnancy and abortion are not proved by any other witness except prosecutrix and medical evidence is also contrary to the statement of prosecutrix, offence under Section

313 is not made out.

In *Asgarali Pradhania vs. Emperor* [22], it was held that saving grace of the offence in each case is good faith and life saving necessity. Accused, with the intention of causing miscarriage and administering harmless substance, is guilty of attempt to cause miscarriage.

According to Crime in India (2000), foeticide cases reported an increase by 49.2 percent over the previous year and infanticide cases increased by over 19.5 percent as compared to the previous year. However, state-wise analysis reveals a wide variation from state to state. Not a single case of foeticide or infanticide has been reported from Arunachal Pradesh, Goa, Himachal Pradesh, Manipur, Mizoram, Nagaland, Tripura and surprisingly even Uttar Pradesh. It is worthwhile exploring why crimes against the born and the unborn do not exist in some states and why some states have reported only infanticide cases or only foeticide cases. These are some of the issues that need to be looked into. Among the states/Union Territories (coming directly under the central government rule) that report prevalence of both infanticide and foeticide, the highest rate of prevalence is found in the states of Maharashtra, followed by Madhya Pradesh, Andhra Pradesh, Rajasthan, Haryana, Bihar and the Union Territory of Delhi.

Mentioning the efforts of women groups in Rajasthan and Tamil Nadu and the Forum against Sex Determination and Sex Pre-selection [23], these groups not only highlighted the utter powerlessness of women who opt for sex linked abortions but have also brought about a significant qualitative change in the consciousness of the decision-making bodies (state, government organisations and non-governmental organisations) by highlighting pertinent issues such as:

1. Economists who apply the law of demand and supply and recommend that the reduction in the 'supply' of women will enhance their status, need to review the anthropological evidence that shows that the regions in India where the sex

ratio is extremely adverse are notorious for some of the most inhuman practices against women. These include forced polyandry, gang rape, abduction, dowry, murders, and the degraded status of widows and deserted women.

2. Techno-doctors who promote non-reproductive technologies for commercial reasons cash in on anti-women biases that reduce the Indian women to a "male child producing machine". They treat a healthy woman as raw material, not as a human being, converting her into a pathological case. They violate the code of medical ethics by violating women's dignity and bodily integrity and also become a party to aiding and abetting the process.
3. Advocates of population control whose target is to achieve a net reproductive rate of zero (NRR-0) by supporting foeticide and whose cynical logic is "fewer women = lesser procreation" have placed Indian women in the category of "endangered species".

Another effort by a voluntary organisation in Tamil Nadu has been reported by Giriraj who conducted the study in Kadayampatti Panchayat of Salem district on 42 families identified by a voluntary organisation 'World Vision' as rescued families who were provided facilities, assistance and awareness with a view to set their mind against female infanticide. His study revealed that 63.91 percent of the respondents were in the age group of 20-30 years and 26.19 percent were above 30 years. Of these, only 19.05 percent of the respondents were married at the age of 19 years and above.

Majority of them, married between 16-18 years (52.38 percent), and (28.57 percent) below 15 years. A large majority (95.24 percent) had nuclear families and nearly two-third (71.43 percent) had 2-3 girl children. The women respondents reported facing problem in the family and psychological disturbance because of giving birth to the girl child and regretted being women. Girl child was considered a liability by 90.48 percent of them though interestingly none of them thought educating the girl was unnecessary in spite of the fact that their own educational background was very dismal, 83.33 percent were illiterate. Employment status showed that more than half (52.38 percent) worked as coolies whereas 42.86 percent were unemployed.

The monthly earnings in majority of the cases ranged between ₹ 1,000-₹2,000. Almost all the respondents stated that burden of dowry and poverty were the two main reasons for female infanticide however, 76.19 percent stated fear of safety for the girl as a reason for female infanticide and 83.33 percent accepted son preference because it is the male who carries the family lineage. An overwhelming majority (83.33 percent) of the respondents believed that they would have committed female infanticide if the voluntary organisation would not have intervened and provided economic assistance/incentives and awareness. Only 4.76 percent of the respondents said that they were afraid of the laws enacted by the government. Most of the women reported that they killed their babies under pressure from their husbands. Many a time the husbands would beat up their wives and force them to kill the female child because she is an economic burden. Such situations occur more so among poverty stricken families. It has been stated that, "the spectre of domestic violence chokes their voice and silences their opposition to attitudes and practices derogatory to their dignity. This social reality does not allow women to protest against any suggestion or coercion to get the female child aborted. It is unthinkable that any woman would readily agree to be a party to the crime. They do so under male pressure, coercion and domination". [24]

4.8 Factors Responsible for Female Foeticide

Increased availability of advanced technologies, especially ultrasonography (USG), has been the single most important factor responsible for decrease in sex ratios and increase in female foeticides. In India, over 25,000 pre-natal units have been registered. [25] Facilities of sex determination through clinic next door, are now conveniently available with the families willing to dish out any amount that is demanded of them. The easy availability of mobile scanning machines has translated into brisk business for doctors. Sex selection techniques became popular in the western and north-western states in the late 1970s and early 1980s whilst they are becoming popular in the South now. [26] The sex of a foetus can be determined at 13-14 weeks of pregnancy by trans-vaginal sonography and by 14-16 weeks through abdominal ultrasound. These methods have rendered early sex determination inexpensive, feasible and easily accessible. Although various preconception techniques that help in choosing the foetal sex have been described, their use is not widespread due to higher costs. [27]

Other factors in this regard are as under:

- The preference for boy in society is so strong that many women choose to abort rather than give birth to a girl.
- There is also religious faith that parents want a son. This is because only male children can perform the last rites for their parents.
- In India, a preference for sons is influenced by social and economic factors.
- Parent's desire sons because they carry on the family name and inherit family property.
- In the absence of social welfare plans, sons are often considered (rightly or wrongly) to be the sole means of support for aging parents.
- The high costs of providing a dowry means daughters are often viewed as *paraya dhan* (to be married and sent away)—another reason why females are singled out for abortion: or in its absence, infanticide.
- The tradition of dowry-giving in India has led to a massive amount of violence towards women.
- Dowry was a custom invented by women for women, a marker of their status.
- Women are forced to abort their female foetus owing to family pressure and the practice of dowry is responsible for this.

- Experts also blame decreasing number of girls on the two-child policy heavily promoted throughout the country.
- The perfect family involves one girl and one boy.
- Families are more likely to abort female foetus if the first child is also girl.
- Lack of education and awareness.
- Women are viewed as a liability because they are seen to need protection and because the benefits of investing in them increases for the families into which they are married.
- These factors along with cultural and religious beliefs constitute the root causes for why sons are preferred and why daughters are not desired.
- Misplaced archaic cultural (nonsense) of girls being the 'honour' of the family. Sadly, this is true for a majority of cultures around the world, but some take it seriously enough to resort to murderous acts for the sake of 'honour' that is driven by super-sized inflatable male chauvinist egos.

In India, the policy environment is supportive of the reproductive choices of women and men. The medical termination of pregnancy act is legal and it allows for induced abortions where pregnancy carries grave injury to women's health. A negative outcome of the PNDT Act was that the practice of sex determination was driven nonetheless and the availability of services proliferated correspondingly. Ultra sound machines continued to be widely available and simple to use. In such an environment, it is very difficult to enforce a law which sought to control information that travels through informal channels and can operate secretly. Law cannot control the information that is conveyed through a mere smile or frown face. Other reasons for limited effectiveness of the law include lack of political will to ensure enforcement. Experience has shown that in general, the role of legislation in subverting a social practice is limited.

The barbaric acts that are committed against women are endless and there is no single cause behind these issues. The secondary status of women and the fact that she is considered nothing more than a commodity has a significant role to play behind the imbalance in male-female sex ratio. Girls are discriminated right from the beginning, even before they are born. India, unfortunately, is one of the countries where female foeticide is on the rise. Government and judiciary have tried working in this direction so that they can get rid of this menace but the results have been far from being satisfactory.

Endnotes

1. Fatima Ehtesham Saddiqi and Sarala Ranganathan, "Handbook on Women and Human Rights: A Guide for Social Activists", Part 1, Kanishka Publishers and Distributors, Delhi, 2001, p. 115.
2. United Nations, "World Population Prospects, 2010".
3. D.D.R. Sachdeva, "Social Welfare Administration in India", Kitab Mahal, Allahabad, 1998, p. 285.
4. S. Bose and K. Trent, "Socio-Demographic Determinants of Abortion in India: A North-South Comparison", Department of Sociology, State University of New York, US, 2006.
5. Leela L. Visaria, "The Declining Sex Ratio in India", *National Media Journal India*, 2004.
6. J.G. Raymond, "In Women as Wombs", *Spinifex*, Melbourne, 1994.
7. S.P. Srivastava, "The Perils of Pre-Birth Murder: A Sociological Analysis of Female Foeticide", *Journal of Social Welfare*, Vol. No. 47, 2001, pp. 7-12.
8. S Bandyopadhyay and A Singh, "History of Son Preference and Sex Selection in India", *The Western Bulletin,* Indian Institute History Medicine, Hyderabad, 2003.
9. B. Miller, "The Endangered Sex: Neglect of Female Children in Rural North India", *Ithaca,* New York and London, Cornell University Press, 1981.
10. Raj Kumar, "Women and Society", Anmol Publications Pvt. Ltd., 2000, p. 33.
11. Shobha Saxena, "Crimes Against Women and Protection Laws", Deep & Deep Publishers, 1995, p. 29.
12. Dr. (Smt.) Sarojini Saxena, "Femijuris", India Publishing Company, 1994, p. 29.

13. Amniocentesis is a procedure used to diagnose foetal defects in the early second trimester of pregnancy. A sample of the amniotic fluid, which surrounds a foetus in the womb, is collected through a pregnant woman's abdomen using a needle and syringe. Tests performed on foetal cells found in the sample can reveal the presence of many types of genetic disorders, thus allowing doctors and prospective parents to make important decisions about early treatment and intervention.
14. A prenatal test to detect birth defects at an early stage of pregnancy; tissue from the chorionic villi is assayed.
15. A diagnostic imaging technique utilizing reflected high frequency sound waves to delineate, measure, or examine internal body structures or organs.
16. http://www.studymode.com/essays/Female-Foeticide-377153.html, last visited on 9th February, 2013.
17. A.I.R., 1935, Cal. 489.
18. Dr. (Smt.) Sarojini Saxena, "Femijuris", India Publishing Company, 1994, pp. 32-33.
19. A.I.R., 1952, M.B. 124.
20. 1960, M.P.L.J.N. 227.
21. 1991(1), M.P.W.N. 91.
22. A.I.R., 1933, Cal. 893.
23. V. Patel, "Indian Women's Struggle to Survive: Campaign Against Foeticide", in The Child and The Law, New Delhi, UNICEF, 1994, pp. 60-61.
24. S.P. Srivastava, "The Perils of Pre-Birth Murder: A Sociological Analysis of Female Foeticide", *Journal of Social Welfare,* Vol. 47, January 2001, pp. 7-12.
25. "Genocide of Indian Daughters", Mail Online, 2006, available at: http://www.dailymail.co.uk/news/article-393896/Genocide-Indiasdaughters.html, last visited on 25th January, 2013.
26. S.M. George, "Sex Selection and Determination in India: Contemporary Developments", *Reproduction and Health Matters*, 2002.
27. M. Gurung, "Female Foeticide", 1999, available at: http://www.hsph.harvard.edu/Organizations/healthnet/SAsia/forums/foeticide/articles/foeticide.html, last visited on 1st April, 2013.

5

Protection of the Girl Child

The Constitution of India has laid special emphasis on the well-being and protection of the children. It not only grants equality and prohibits any kind of discrimination but also protects children against exploitation and abuse. It also empowers the State to adopt measures of positive discrimination in favour of children.

The care and focus given to a child as a girl and as an adolescent—with focus on her health and nutrition, education and economic potential—determines her empowerment as a woman. A healthy, literate and empowered adolescent girl is able to contribute positively to the society.

India ratified the UN Convention on the Rights of the Child in 1992 and formulated the National Plan of Action for Children in the same year. The period 1991-2000 was also observed as the 'SAARC Decade of the Girl Child'. The commitments at the international and national levels have translated into a specific focus on the development of the girl child and adolescent girls, especially on their survival, health, education and protection. The Tenth Five Year Plan (2002-07), viewed the development of children not merely as the most desirable investment for the country's future.

5.1 Right to Life of Girl Child's

The Central Social Welfare Board and State Boards launched a year-long awareness drive on Human Rights Day (December 10, 2003) against female foeticide and celebrated this day as 'Manvi Sanrakshan Diwas' (Protection of Women Day). The objective of the drive was to make people aware of the seriousness of the problem and to generate consciousness against sex selection through workshops, seminars, rallies, print and audio visual campaigns. Key target groups identified were women groups, self-help groups (SHGs), youth groups, medical practitioners, resident welfare associations in urban areas and panchayats in rural areas.

Mass communication media are widely used for disseminating messages condemning female foeticide. Government of India launched the 'Save the Girl Child Campaign' with a view to lessen son preference by highlighting achievements of young girls.

Responding to the declining sex ratio as a social problem, the *Akal Takth*—the highest seat of spiritual and temporal authority amongst Sikhs—issued a *hukumnama* (diktat) on April 6, 2001, prohibiting pre-natal sex determination to stop the practice of female foeticide.

The state of Goa has introduced a landmark legislation for the protection of children, particularly to ensure elimination of all forms of discrimination against the girl child and to prevent pre-natal sex selection and female foeticide and female infanticide and foeticide. The Goa Children Act, 2003 seeks to protect the rights of the child, and gives special attention to the needs of the girl child and the elimination of all gender biases. It bans child prostitution and all forms of trafficking of girl child and sexual abuse.

The *Janani Suraksha* Scheme (revamped National Maternity Benefit Scheme) is a package of services geared at reducing maternal mortality, neo-natal mortality, female foeticide and gender disparity. It also aims at improving registration of births and deaths, amongst most disadvantaged strata of population, by increasing access to institutional delivery.

Under the scheme, pregnant women get ₹ 500 after delivery of a male child and ₹ 1,000 after delivery of a female child. A National Commitment Campaign was launched on the occasion of World Population Day on July 11, 2003 focussing on two key elements—safe motherhood and adolescence. It included a signature campaign by students, politicians, sports persons and film stars in favour of the slogan, *beti ho ya beta, rakhein parivar chota* (whether boy or girl, keep family small).

In addition to legal action and awareness campaigns, *Balika Samriddhi Yojana* was launched in 1997 to help in raising the overall status of the girl child and bring about a positive change in family and community attitudes. A cash grant of ₹ 500 is made to the mother of a girl (up to 2 per mother) and a further amount is invested in a financial instrument for education of the girl child and to make her economically independent. This is paid to the girl when she attains the age of 18 years and remains unmarried till then. In addition, the girl child is entitled to receive a scholarship for each class of study, successfully completed.

5.2 Childhood Malnutrition

Adolescent girls are highly susceptible to anaemia which is responsible for miscarriage, still births, premature births, low birth weight babies and maternal mortality during child birth. Girls need 10 percent more iron than boys for biological reasons. Studies undertaken to develop National Strategy for Reducing Childhood Malnutrition under the Regional Technical Assistance programme of Asian Development Bank identified female illiteracy, age at marriage of girls and age at the first child birth as the critical determinants of malnutrition and low birth weight in newborns which directly and indirectly influence infant and maternal mortality rates.

The Government's Integrated Child Development Services (ICDS) programme, the world's largest early childcare and development programme, reaches 34 million children aged 0-6 years and 7 million pregnant and nursing mothers.

Interventions include training of *Anganwadi* (childcare) workers, improved communication strategies, improved monitoring and reporting systems, provision of essential supplies, and development of community-based early childcare interventions.

The *Pradhan Mantri Gramoday Yojana*, started in 2000-

01, has nutrition as one of its components which caters to children in the age group of 6-36 months so as to prevent the onset of under-nutrition in that age group.

As part of the ICDS programme, the *Kishori Shakti Yojana*, an intervention for adolescent girls (11-18 years) was launched in 2000-01. The scheme is currently being implemented in 2,000 blocks across the country. This intervention seeks to address the needs of adolescents for self-development, nutrition and health status, literacy and numerical skills, vocational skills etc.

5.3 Education and Schooling

Under the *Sarva Shiksha Abhiyan* (Education for All), specific strategies have been designed to enhance girls access, enrolment and schooling. The recently launched National Plan for Education at the Elementary Level (NPEGEL), an integral part of the SSA, provides a dynamic framework for accelerating progress in girls' education.

Innovative approaches to encouraging and ensuring equality in access to education for girls include residential bridge courses. Iron and folic acid supplementation of adolescent girls is being undertaken in the World Bank assisted ICDS projects and also under the Reproductive and Child Health Programme of Department of Family Welfare on a pilot scale. Micro-nutrient supplements are provided to adolescent girls through ICDS in 4 States in collaboration with the Micro-nutrient Initiative.

5.4 Sexual Abuse and Trafficking

Young girls are especially vulnerable to sexual abuse and trafficking. The Supreme Court of India has issued fresh guidelines for the trial of child abuse cases, aimed at protecting victims from being harassed during trial. Expressing concern over increasing incidence of crimes against children, the court suggested the enactment of stricter legislation to punish child-sex offenders.

In-camera trials, previously permitted only in rape cases, are now available in cases of child abuse and violence. The revamped Juvenile Justice Act, 2000 assures that the child in need of care and protection as per the Act is defined to cover those found vulnerable and likely to be inducted into drug abuse or trafficking. Section 23 provides for punishment to a person having actual charge of or control over a child and who assaults, abandons or wilfully neglects the child or causes or procures him to be assaulted, abandoned, exposed or neglected in a manner likely to cause unnecessary mental or physical suffering. In addition, Section 24 provides for punishment for employment or use of a child for begging. Section 25 provides for penalty for giving intoxicating liquor or narcotic drug or psychotropic substance to a child.

5.5 Measures to Protect the Girl Child

The persistence of poverty, discriminatory attitudes towards women and girls, negative cultural attitudes and practices against girls have contributed to a lack of opportunities for girls to become confident and self-reliant, and independent adults.

5.5.1 Dhanalakshmi: This is a Central sector scheme, fully funded by the Centre, which attempts to tackle the acute problem of declining sex ratio. It was launched in 2008 to bring about a change in the mindset of the family towards the girl child. It provides cash transfers to the family of the girl child (preferably the mother) on fulfilment of certain conditionalities like birth registration, immunisation, enrolment and retention in school and marriage after attaining the age of 18 years. An amount of ₹ 5,000 is provided at registration of birth; ₹ 1,000 on enrolment for education; and ₹ 6,250 is provided in varying instalments as her education proceeds. The total amount provided to the beneficiary is ₹ 13,500, along with an insurance cover. The scheme is in operation on a pilot basis in 11 blocks across seven states; Andhra Pradesh, Bihar, Chhattisgarh, Odisha, Jharkhand, Punjab and Uttar Pradesh.

5.5.2 Prevention of Child Pornography: On January 30, 1997, the United Nations General Assembly adopted, through a Resolution, the Model Law on Electronic Commerce adopted by the United Nations Commission on International Trade Law. This is referred to as the UNCITRAL Model Law on E-Commerce.

Following the UN Resolution, the Indian Parliament passed the Information Technology Act (ITA), 2000 in May 2000 and notified it for effectiveness on October 17, 2000.

ITA, 2000 was substantially amended through the Information Technology Amendment Act, 2008 which was passed by the two houses of the Indian Parliament on December 23 and 24, 2008. It got the Presidential assent on February 5, 2009 and was notified for effectiveness on October 27, 2009.

Section 67B—a new section added in the ITA, 2008—deals with child pornography. It states: whoever,

(a) publishes or transmits or causes to be published or transmitted material in any electronic form which depicts children engaged in sexually explicit act or conduct, or;
(b) creates text or digital images, collects, seeks, browses, downloads, advertises, promotes, exchanges or distributes material in any electronic form depicting children in obscene or indecent or sexually explicit manner, or;
(c) cultivates, entices or induces children to online relationship with one or more children for and on sexually explicit act or in a manner that may offend a reasonable adult on the computer resource, or;
(d) facilitates abusing children online, or;
(e) records in any electronic form own abuse or that of others pertaining to sexually explicit act with children;

shall be punished on first conviction with imprisonment of either description for a term which may extend to five years and with a fine which may extend to ₹ 10 lakh and in the event of second or subsequent conviction with imprisonment of either description for a term which may extend to seven years and also with fine which may extend to ₹ 10 lakh.

Provided that the provisions of this section do not extend to any book, pamphlet, paper, writing, drawing, painting, representation or figure in electronic form:

(i) the publication of which is proved to be justified as being for the public good on the ground that such book, pamphlet, paper writing, drawing, painting, representation or figure is in the interest of science, literature, art or learning or other objects of general concern, or;

(ii) which is kept or used for bonafide heritage or religious purposes

Explanation: For the purposes of this section, "children" means a person who has not completed the age of 18 years.

5.6 United Nations Convention on the Rights of the Child (UNCRC)

The United Nations Convention on the Rights of the Child (UNCRC) is an international human rights treaty that grants all children and young people (aged 17 and under), a comprehensive set of rights. The UK signed the Convention on 19th April, 1990, ratified it on 16th December, 1991 and it came into force on 15th January, 1992.

The UNCRC is presently the most widely ratified international human rights treaty. It is the only international human rights treaty to include civil, political, economic, social and cultural rights. It sets out in detail what every child needs to have a safe, happy and fulfilled childhood regardless of their sex, religion, social origin, and where and to whom they were born. All United Nations member states, except for the United States and Somalia, have ratified the Convention.

The Convention gives children and young people, over 40 substantive rights, including the right to:

- Special protection measures and assistance.
- Access to services such as education and healthcare.
- Develop their personalities, abilities and talents to the fullest potential.

- Grow up in an environment of happiness, love and understanding.
- Be informed about and participate in achieving their rights in an accessible and active manner.

The Government is committed to the UNCRC and to its implementation. As a state party, the Westminster Government is responsible for the overall coordination of the UNCRC across the UK. The Department for Education is the lead department with responsibility for implementing the UNCRC in England and for coordinating UK-wide reports, although each of the devolved administrations implements the UNCRC and addresses the Committee's recommendations as appropriate to their own local requirements.

The UK Government submitted its consolidated third and fourth reports to the UN Committee on 15th July, 2007, setting out details on progress made against the Convention since the previous reports.

6

Legislative Efforts to Combat Female Foeticide

6.1 Policy Framework

National Plan of Action exclusively for the girl child (1991-2000) was formulated in 1992 for the 'Survival, Protection and Development of the Girl Child'. The Plan recognized the rights of the girl child to equal opportunity, to be free from hunger, illiteracy, ignorance and exploitation. Towards ensuring survival of the girl child, the objectives are, to:

1. Prevent cases of female foeticide and infanticide and ban the practice of amniocentesis for sex determination;
2. End gender disparity in infant mortality rate; eliminate gender disparities in feeding practices, expand nutritional interventions to reduce severe malnourishment by half and provide supplementary nutrition to adolescent girls in need;
3. Reduce deaths due to diarrhoea by 50 percent among girl children under 5 years and ensure immunization against all forms of serious illnesses; and
4. Provide safe drinking water and ensure access to fodder and drinking water near home.

The launching of the *Balika Samriddhi Yojana* in 1997 is a major initiative of the Government to raise the overall status of the girl child. It intends to change family and community attitudes towards her and her mother. Under this scheme, about 25 lakh girl children born every year in families below the poverty line are to be benefited. The first component of the scheme, which has already been launched, is to provide ₹ 500 as a post-delivery grant to the mother of the girl child as a symbolic gift from the Government. The other components proposed under the scheme include (a) provision of annual scholarships to the beneficiaries when they go to school and (b) assistance for taking upon income generating activity when they attain the age of maturity.

Besides having specific legislations and policy proclamations to deal with this menace, the precipitating factors such as dowry, poverty, and woman's economic dependence etc., leading to the problem of foeticide and infanticide have been addressed by enacting various legislations like:

1. Dowry Prohibition Act, 1961 (amended in 1986).
2. Hindu Marriage Act, 1955.
3. Hindu Adoption and Maintenance Act, 1956.
4. Immoral Traffic Prevention Act, 1986.
5. Equal Remuneration Act, 1976.

These and various other legislations and policy proclamations intend to bring about women's economic and social empowerment to the maximum and it is hoped that such measures would equip women to exercise their rights.

6.2 Right Per Se of the Foetus

Regard for sanctity of the embryo from the moment of conception is enjoined by the Hindu Scriptures. Thus, the destruction of a foetus is condemned as a heinous offence equal to *Brahmahatya.* In this condemnation, no distinction appears to have been made between different stages of gestation. The *Garbhoponishad*, which gives a meticulous account of the development of the foetus from the moment of conception of the mother, states that from the second day after the entry of the male semen into the female uterus, the semen gets thickened and from the 8th day, it takes the shape of a ball which is transformed into a lump after 15 days, leading to the creation of the head and the legs after two months. It follows, that it would be an offence if the embryo is destroyed even at the nascent stage.

In Re. A.C, it was held by the court that the state has an important and legitimate interest in protecting the potentiality of human life, when the foetus has become viable. It had also been acknowledged earlier in *Roe vs. Wade* that State's interest in potential human life becomes compelling at a point of viability. This is a situation, which exists when a woman has carried an unborn child to viability, and when the unborn child reaches this stage, the child becomes a party, whose interest must be considered. A similar approach has been adopted by the courts in *Fowler vs. Woodward* and more recently in *Whitner vs. South Carolina.* In all these cases, it was opined that 'viable foetuses' are 'persons' in the eyes of law, certain legal rights and privileges and exclusion of viable foetus from status of person would be an "unsound, illogical and unjust". It was unanimously held that a foetus having reached that period of prenatal maturity where it is capable of independent life apart from its mother, is a person.

After the perusal of the above-mentioned cases, it would be safe to conclude that a foetus has a legal status of a fully born person in the eyes of law. And therefore, state's interest in protecting the life and health of the viable foetuses is not merely legitimate but compelling.

In cases where the woman is pregnant and she cannot have normal vaginal delivery, the only option left to the doctors after detailed medical prognosis is the caesarean section. If the woman consents to the operation, there is no problem but if she refuses and her refusal may prove fatal to the foetus, then in such a case the right to life of the valid and recognized legal person would be infringed. This is based upon a simple logic that the foetus is a 'person' in eyes of law and as such it carries with it all rights vested in a person, including the right to life. And if such a right is infringed, the court through '*court-ordered caesarean section*' could well enforce it.

That the existing law of India in the Penal Code, enacted as early as 1860, acknowledges that an embryo is entitled to legal protection of the unborn child's right to life, is evident from Section 315. Section 312 of the Indian Penal Code provides punishment of imprisonment of either description for a term which may extend to seven years, and shall also be liable to fine the woman causing miscarriage of a child. By treating the act of procuring an abortion as an offence, an implicit protection has been provided to the foetal right. Section 20 of the Hindu Succession Act, 1956 has conferred a right to succeed to the father's estate on a child who was in the mother's womb when the father died intestate. Under Section 3 of the Medical Termination of Pregnancy, 1971, abortion is allowed only under certain circumstances, for example, continuance of pregnancy would risk life of the pregnant woman or there is a substantial risk of physical or mental abnormalities in the unborn child.

Pre-Conception and Pre-Natal Diagnostic Techniques (Prohibition of Sex Selection) Act, 1994 prohibits the pre-natal tests of sex determination of the foetus, through which unborn female child could be protected. After expiry of three months, the foetus then presumably has the 'capability of meaningful life outside the mother's womb' and this stage is known as "quickening" i.e., when the foetus first starts recognizable movements in the uterus. At this stage, the state acquires compelling interest to protect the potential. Article 2 of the West German Constitution, 1949, states as under:

1. Everyone shall have the right to the free development of his personality insofar as it does not violate the rights of the others or offend against the constitutional order or the moral code.
2. Everyone shall have the right to life and to inviolability of his person. The liberty of the individual shall be inviolable. These rights may only be encroached upon pursuant to a law.

In *Abortion Reform Law Case*, the West German Constitutional Court laid down the following proposition:

1. "Everyone" in Article 2 includes an unborn being;
2. Human life exists in embryo from the fourteenth day of the conception;
3. It is the duty of the state to protect and promote the life of the foetus and defend it from unlawful interference by other person;
4. The right of development accrues in the foetus from the

mother's womb and is not complete even after birth;

5. If the foetus was considered only as a part of the maternal organism, termination of pregnancy would remain entirely in the sphere of private life, not warranting public interferences. But because the foetus is "an autonomous human being" under protection of the constitution, termination of pregnancy has a social dimension which demands public regulation;
6. The constitution also protects a woman's right to free development of her personality, which includes freedom to decide against parenthood. But this right is not guaranteed without limitations. The right of others, the constitutional order, and the moral code all restrict it;
7. A compromise which guarantees, both protection of foetus as well as the freedom of abortion of a pregnant woman, is impossible because termination of pregnancy always means "destruction of unborn life". The legal order cannot, therefore, make a woman's self determination, the principle of its regulations. On the other hand, protection of foetus must be given priority to the woman's right of self-determination;
8. The state is to effectively fulfil its duty to 'protect' a "developing life". In discharging this duty, the state is to make a reasonable adjustment between the unborn right to life and woman's right to her own life and health. The unborn's right to life can lead to burdens for the woman which sharply exceed those of a normal pregnancy. In such a case, the state may exempt the pregnant woman from punishment for destroying the foetus where it is necessary to protect the pregnant woman from a threat to her life or a threat of a serious impact on her health or other cases, where the burden is extraordinary; and
9. The duty of the court is not to put itself in the legislator's place, but to determine whether the legislator has fulfilled its duty to protect the "developing life" and made a reasonable adjustment between the right of the unborn and

the right of the pregnant woman".

Article 40(3) of the Constitution of Eire (inserted in 1983) enjoins the state to reconcile the right to life of an unborn child with the right to life of the mother. Hence, where the abortion was not required to save the life of the mother, damages or injunction may be available to protect the unborn child. In US, following propositions may be deduced so far from the judicial decisions as regards the status of the foetus:

- The word 'person' in the 14th Amendment means a human being after birth and not foetus. It follows that the right to life does not begin from the conception.
- It cannot be denied, however that there is a potentiality of life in the embryo from the moment of conception, so that the state may take this into consideration in regulating the mother's right to abortion.

The American Supreme Court has introduced the test of 'viability', according to the period of pregnancy. (i) During the first three months of pregnancy, the potentiality of life in the embryo is not viable and abortion at this stage is less risky or fatal to the mother. Hence, the state may refrain from exercising its right of regulation of the mother's right to abortion, leaving it to be the decision of the mother and her physician. (ii) After the expiry of three months, however, "the foetus then presumably has the capability of meaningful life outside the mother's womb". This stage is otherwise known as 'quickening', i.e., when the foetus first starts recognizable movement in the uterus. At this stage, therefore, the state acquires compelling interest to protect the potential.

Roe vs. Wade [1] is one of the most controversial and politically significant cases in the US Supreme Court history. In this, the Constitutional validity of state criminal abortion legislation was considered, which prohibited abortion except by medical advice for the purpose of saving the mother. It was contended that a woman's right to terminate the pregnancy is absolute and that she is entitled to terminate the pregnancy for whatever reason she chooses. The court upheld the right to privacy, but at the same time held that the same is not absolute and that the state can interfere and regulate the freedom for 'compelling state interests'.

It was held that the child birth endangers the lives of some women, voluntary abortion 'at any time and place' regardless of medical standards would impinge on a rightful concern of the society. The woman's health is part of that concern as is the life of the foetus after quickening. These concerns justify the state in treating the procedure as a medical one. In *Webster vs. Reproductive Health Services et al.*, the court was asked to decide the constitutionality of Missouri Statute regulating the performance of abortion. In the preamble of the Statute, it was provided "that life of each human being begins at conception" and that "unborn children have protectable interests in life, health and well-being" and required that all state laws be interpreted to provide unborn children with the same rights enjoyed by the persons, subject to the federal constitution. The court decided that the preamble simply expressed a value judgment without going into its constitutionality.

The provision in the Act which prohibited any public employee within the scope of his employment to perform or assist an abortion, not necessary to save the life of the mother was held valid. In its lesser known companion case, *Doe vs. Bolton* [1], it was decided at the same time, that a mother may abort her pregnancy for any reason, up until the "point at which foetus becomes "viable". The court defined viable as, being "potentially able to live outside the mother's womb, albeit with artificial aid. Viability is usually placed at about seven months (28 weeks) but may occur earlier, even at 24 weeks." The Court also held that abortion after viability must be available when needed to protect women's health, which the court defined broadly in the companion case *Doe vs. Bolton*. These rulings affected laws in 46 states.

In India, two acts deal with the issue of female foeticide:

- Medical Termination of Pregnancy Act, 1971, and
- Pre Natal Diagnostic Techniques (Regulation and Prevention of Misuse) Act, 1994.

6.3 Medical Termination of Pregnancy Act, 1971

Taking note of the dismal state of affairs, the central Family Planning Board persuaded the Central Government to appoint a committee known as Shantilal Committee in the year 1964. The recommendations of this committee culminated in the enactment of the Medical Termination of Pregnancy Act, 1971. Abortion was legalized only in 1971 when this Act was passed. The Medical Termination of Pregnancy bill was passed by both the houses of the Parliament and received the assent of the President of India on 10th August, 1971. This law guarantees the right of abortion to women in India to terminate an unintended pregnancy by a registered medical practitioner in a hospital established or maintained by the government or a place being approved for the purpose of this Act by the government. Not all pregnancies could be terminated under the Act.

The object of the Act, besides being the elimination of the high incidence of illegal abortions, is perhaps to confer on the woman, the right to privacy, [2] which includes the right to space and to limit pregnancies (i.e. whether or not to bear children) and the right to decide about her own body. [3] Another important feature of the Act is to encourage a reduction in the rate of population growth by permitting termination of an unwanted pregnancy on the ground that a contraceptive device failed. [4]

The Act in a way, liberalized the abortion policy, as pregnancy could be terminated:

- As a health measure, where the continuance of pregnancy involves as a risk:
  -to the life of the pregnant woman, or
  -of grave injury to her physical or mental health. [5]
- On humanitarian grounds, where pregnancy is a result of sexual violence.
- On eugenic grounds, where the child to be born is likely to suffer from such physical or mental abnormalities as to be seriously handicapped.

The Act legalizes the abortion by qualified professionals on humanitarian or medical grounds. The maximum punishment may go up to life imprisonment. The Act has been further amended, specifying the place and persons authorized to perform abortion and provides for penal actions against the unauthorized persons performing abortions.

The Act no doubt diluted the provisions of the IPC. The only caution, which the statute took care of, was the termination of pregnancy on any of the grounds as mentioned above could be done only by a registered medical practitioner. This was supposed to be a safeguard against female mortality but it paved way for unintended results. Those desirous of effecting female foeticide invoked this Act to effect selective abortion. Coupled with this situation was the clandestine practice of some recalcitrant quacks aborting female foetuses under cover. Thus, this latest technology proved to be a useful tool in the hands of these unscrupulous people, even miscarriage was affected by quacks and the courts including Supreme Court seemed to look at it casually. In *Jacob George vs. State of Kerala* [6], a homeopath that caused miscarriage of a woman was sentenced to 5 years imprisonment and ₹ 1,000 was imposed as fine by the Kerala High Court. On an appeal, the Supreme Court revised it by imposing a fine of ₹ 1 lakh. If the accused was not to pay the fine, the sentence imposed by the Kerala High Court was to be revived.

Meanwhile, there was a sustained campaign by the Forum against Sex Determination and Sex Pre Selection (FASDSP) and other action groups against the practice, due to excessive female foeticide in northern and western states of India. There were strong protests and agitations to curb the evil practice of female foeticide. In order to arrest this trend, which had tremendous potential to thwart the female sex ratio, essential for the healthy existence of the society, the Pre Natal Diagnostic Techniques (Regulation and Prevention of Misuse) Act, 1994 (PNDT) was enacted. This Act came into force from January 1, 1996. In fact, it was the state of Maharashtra which took the initiative in 1988 to enact the Maharashtra Regulation of Pre Natal Diagnostic Techniques Act. Subsequently, the need for a central legislation with stringent provisions was strongly felt. A bill was introduced in 1991 in the Lok Sabha but people whose business flourished out of this practice, opposed it. The plea of failure of family planning programme was also taken but despite all this opposition, the Bill was passed. The Act has two aspects:

- **Regulatory:** It seeks to regulate the use of pre-natal diagnostic techniques for legal or medical purposes.
- **Preventive:** It prevents misuse for illegal purposes.

The Act provides for the setting up of various bodies along with their composition, powers and functions. There is a central supervisory board, appropriate authorities and advisory committees.

From the bare reading of the Act, it becomes clear that the Medical Termination of Pregnancy Act does not encompass a fundamental right to induce abortion but is limited to liberalization of the conditions under which women may have access to abortion services provided by approved medical practitioners. Medical liberalization, therefore, necessitates mediatisation of the liberalized conditions given in the Act.

6.4 Right to Abort vs. Right of an Unborn

The abortion debate refers to discussion and controversy surrounding the moral and legal status of abortion. The two main groups involved in the abortion debate include the pro choice and pro life supporters, which generally supports access to abortion and regards it as morally wrong. Each movement has varying results and different opinions, as for example in Canada, abortion is available on demand while in Nicaragua abortions are illegal.

Pro Choice: Pro choice describes the political and ethical view that a woman should have complete control over her fertility and the choice to continue or terminate a pregnancy. This entails the guarantee of reproductive rights, which include access to sexual education. Individuals and organizations that support these positions make up the pro choice movement.

Pro Life: It is a term representing a variety of prospective and activist movements in bio ethics. It most commonly refers to opposition to abortion and support for foetal rights. The term describes the political and ethical view which maintains that foetuses and embryos are human beings and therefore have a right to live.

As said earlier, the Constitution of India provides for right to life and liberty under Article 21 and this concept of liberty subsumes within itself, certain unremunerated rights, which are essential to human dignity. One such right is the right to privacy i.e. an individual has an absolute control over his body and no one can interfere with his bodily integrity except with his/her permission. Similarly, the courts have recognized that a foetus is a person in the eyes of law and as such it enjoys all the privileges and rights enjoyed by a human being. With the expansive interpretation being given to this right and with the passage of time, various new rights such as right to privacy hitherto not specifically granted under the Constitution were included in the plethora of right available under Article 21.

6.4.1 Compliance with Right to Equality [7]: Since right to life includes right to enjoy life with all the limbs and faculties, therefore the right to procreation and right to have control over reproductive organs are included in the broader concept of right to life. Every person including a girl has a right to marry and thereby to conceive a child which is absolute. Right to procreation and to have control over ones' reproductive organs gives birth to another right i.e. the right to abortion. This raises another peculiar problem of balancing the life and liberty of born and unborn, more so in the present day social structure where female sex ratio has deteriorated. On the one hand, the modern educated woman cries for liberal abortion laws in the name of right to life and personal liberty whereas on the other hand the government has to tighten the screws with a view to curb social tendency to kill female foetus. The issue has therefore, become very complex in the present day social structure.

On a plain reading, nothing in it apart from the word "provided" supports the former argument. The whole argument seems to be rested by the Handbook on the PNDT Act which is published by the Department of Health, Government of India, to aid appropriate authorities in their functioning. The handbook specifically states that the pre-natal diagnostic procedures can only be conducted under the circumstances provided in clause (3).

This is arbitrary and completely goes against the principles of equality. The Act creates a distinction between healthy and unhealthy women for the purposes of pre-natal procedures. This distinction has no bearing upon the issue at hand i.e. the prevention of sex determination.

Although the conditions mentioned in clause (3) significantly increase the chances of a genetic abnormality, a disease of that sort can occur to any foetus, regardless of the toxicity of the pregnant woman's workplace.

The legislature has effectively prohibited the test to be conducted on a significant portion of pregnant women. What the Act says is that if you do not fulfil any one of the conditions laid down in clause (3), you cannot have a test conducted, and would have to bear with the anguish in the chance, albeit a slim one, that the child is born with a genetic abnormality. This distinction has absolutely no bearing on the issue at hand: preventing sex-selection.

6.4.2 Compliance with Right to Privacy [8]: The Indian Constitution does not expressly provide a constitutional right to privacy. It has taken the route of judicial interpretation. The Courts have started defining this right ever since the much-publicized *A.K. Gopalan Case* [9] in 1956. In a recent case, the Court has observed, "as a concept it may be too broad and moralistic to define it judicially. Whether right to privacy can be claimed or has been infringed in a given case would depend on the facts of the case".

In *Roe vs. Wade*, the right to privacy was discussed at a

great length. The honourable judges concluded that a right to privacy did indeed exist. However, the American Bill of Rights expressly provides for a right to sexual privacy. Even without any counterpart, the Indian Courts have deduced a right to "*reproductive autonomy*", as mentioned earlier, over a period of many cases. The Court has gone as far as saying that, "The right to make a decision about reproduction is essentially a very personal decision either on the part of the man or the woman".

Over the times, the Court has repeatedly observed that all matters related to reproduction are a very private matter and cannot be inquired into or regulated by the government. This is known as the "right to reproductive autonomy". Article 8 of the European Convention also talks about right to privacy. The right to privacy basically means a right to be let alone. Strictly in the legal sense, it may be considered that the legislature may, by enacting a law that keeps out of reach many pre-natal procedures to the couple, be infringing upon the privacy of the married couple.

They would, obviously, prefer to keep all matters relating to their procreation and child bearing secret, and would not like the idea of anyone trying to interfere or regulate it, least of all, the Government. Child birth is a very personal issue of the married couple (European thinkers have gone far enough to state that marriage is the means of legally having a child), and the married couple is the sole authority to take all the decisions relating to the child.

The courts have from long shown a tendency to expand the right to privacy of people over the ages. As and when an issue arises as to the scope of privacy, the court has been of the opinion of upholding the right. A few decades ago, abortions were the talk of the academic and moralistic circles, with everyone being divided into pro-life and pro-abortion camps. The courts around the world, most notably America in *Roe vs. Wade*, took the opinion that abortions are a fundamental right. When the issue of contraceptives came around, they too were held to be part of the fundamental rights.

Now the latest controversy is surrounding these diagnostic procedures. Taking a cue from this earlier trend, the court might just extend the canopy of fundamental rights over these too. Going into the more controversial issue of sex-selective abortions, the court possibly may take the opinion that any law banning them is bad for violation of rights. *Roe vs. Wade*, the much publicized American case, already has laid down that the State may interfere with the right to abortion only in some compelling interest of the state, like promoting better health of the woman. In the honourable judge's opinion, no other reason can be provided; although, in our opinion, in our social scenario, the prevailing trends may be considered compelling enough.

Abortion many people believe is a moral issue but it is also a constitutional issue. It is a woman's right to choose what she does with her body and it should not be altered or influenced by anyone else. As submitted above, a girl has an absolute freedom to conceive a child but after she exercises this freedom, termination of foetus becomes an offence under IPC and MTP Act, 1971. There is a perception that UN Declarations and other human, civil and political right conventions and other international instruments do not defend the unborn, but there are equally valid arguments to the contrary.

Firstly, Article 6, para 5, of the International Covenant on Civil and Political Rights, 1966, stipulates that capital punishment cannot be carried on pregnant woman.

Secondly, in many jurisdictions, abortion is as a rule, prohibited and penalized and is permitted only for certain serious reasons and under strict conditions.

Thirdly, in the civil codes of many states, the legal personality of the unborn child is recognized indirectly by the mere fact that the law recognizes the right of the unborn child to inherit, to receive donations and to succeed.

Lastly, para 9 of the Preamble of the Convention on the Rights of the Child states, "bearing in mind that as indicated in the declarations of the rights of the child", "the child reason of his physical and mental immaturity needs special safeguards and care, including appropriate legal protection before as well as after the birth".

Similarly, the American Convention on Human Rights in Article 4, para 1, states, "every person has the right to have life respected. This right shall be protected by law and in general from the moment of conception. No one shall arbitrarily be deprived of his life".

6.4.3 Nikita Case: Niketa and Haresh Mehta, who were married, decided to seek the court's permission to have an abortion when their doctor informed them that the foetus in Niketa's womb had a complete congenital heart block.

Rather than going through with the pregnancy, the couple decided on an abortion only to come up against stipulations in the Medical Termination of Pregnancy Act, 1971, that permits abortions only up to 20 weeks, and that too on certification by at least two medical practitioners that either the mother's or the child's life is at risk.

The Bombay High Court heard the case and denied the petition stating that they could not make an exception in the case and that nothing in the report of the expert committee they had instituted, suggested that the child's life was at risk. They also suggested that the court could not change the law, that this was the job of legislators and that people like Mehta's should seek a change in the law.

The case has thrown up a fascinating number of issues that concerns an individual's choice, ethics, technology and the law. In each instance, there are no clear guidelines; there is nothing that is black and white.

Much of the press coverage, for instance, stressed the right of Niketa as a mother to choose whether she wants to bring this child into the world or not and whether she wants to be burdened with the possibility of a disabled child. There is nothing wrong with this formulation. The battle for women's reproductive rights has rested on the issue of choice. Yet, there are limitations—ethical, scientific and legal.

For example, women groups around the world have fought for liberal abortion laws so that women do not have to put their lives at risk by seeking illegal abortions as a result of unwanted pregnancies. Yet in India, women groups have had to figure out how to prevent a liberal law from being misused for sex-selective abortions. Of course, it could be argued, and indeed has been argued, that this too is a woman's choice. Women prefer not to give birth to girls because they want to spare them the suffering that they are bound to encounter for the rest of their lives as well as the problems they themselves will face as mothers of girls. Yet, the "*choice*" for sex-selective abortions has been denied under the law in India because of the growing evidence of the impact of this on sex ratio in some parts of the country.

Niketa's case also brings into focus the question of the use and misuse of technology. Ultra-sonography and earlier, amniocentesis, were principally meant to detect genetic abnormalities. Yet in India, they have been deliberately and callously misused to detect the sex of the foetus following which women seek an abortion. There would be cases of genetic disorders followed by abortions too but as these are usually detected at a later stage in the pregnancy—as happened to Niketa—legal abortions are not an option.

But, like choice, technology too has a flip side. Thus, while the technology to detect genetic abnormalities has been misused to determine the sex of the child, advances in science today are ensuring that even children born with congenital problems, such as arterial blocks, can actually be treated and can go on to live normal lives. Hence, the same mother who uses technology to ensure that the child in her womb is normal and healthy also has the knowledge that even if there is a problem, there is now a medical solution.

The case has raised legal issues including the need to amend the MTP Act. Those against sex-selective abortions have argued fiercely for maintaining the 20 week limit while others would argue that there is a case for relaxing it by a few weeks. The time limit varies from country to country where abortion is legal. Therefore, there should be no objection to debating the possibility of amending the law.

The liberalized law confers a position of predominance on medical practitioners who mediate women's access to abortion services—pregnancies cannot be terminated in approved centres unless they are authorized by doctors. The two considerations that are brought into are merely the length and type of pregnancy. According to the Act, the termination of pregnancies up to 12 weeks can be authorized by one doctor while those between 12 to 20 weeks necessitate the opinion of two doctors.

The Act also requires that abortion be induced legally only by a registered medical practitioner who has such experience or training in gynaecology and obstetrics and conducted only at a place that is sanctioned by the appropriate authority. This stipulation is essential and laudable. However, a liberalized law has little meaning for many women who wish to terminate their pregnancies in the absence of a well-developed network of abortion facilities. The MTP Act fails to regard the right to access as a justifiable right and is, therefore, ineffectual in curbing the incidence of illegal abortion. [10]

As with the development of technology, it became progressively easier to identify the sex of the foetus at an early stage. PNDT Act began to be deployed for sex selective abortions. The Pre-Natal Diagnostic Techniques (Regulation and Prevention of Misuse) Act was enacted to curb the malpractice of identifying and terminating the foetus.

6.5 Pre-Natal Diagnostic Techniques (Regulation and Prevention of Misuse) Act, 1994

Due to excessive female infanticide in the northern and western states of India, there were strong agitations and protests to curb the evil of female foeticide. The state of Maharashtra became the first state in the country to ban pre-natal sex determination through the enactment of Maharashtra Regulation of PNDT Act. Similar efforts at the national level resulted in the enactment of the central Pre-Natal Diagnostic Techniques (Regulation and Prevention of Misuse) Act, 1994. It was brought into operation on January 1, 1996. The Act prohibits determination and disclosure of the sex of foetus. The Act was amended in the year 2003 to include sex determination at pre-conception stage and action against advertisements promising a male child. The amended Act received the assent of the President of India on 17th January, 2003. The Act is now called PC & PNDT Act (Pre-Conception and Pre-Natal Diagnostic Techniques (Regulation and Prevention of Misuse) Act as amended by Amendment Act of 2002. The statistics given on the first page are a pointer to the fact that the laws governing foeticide make the PNDT Act totally ineffective. The Supreme Court of India in its order dated 4th May, 2001 on the writ petition by an NGO called Centre for Inquiry into Health and Allied Themes (CEHAT) against the Union of India, opined: [11]

"*Prima facie, it appears that despite the PNDT Act being enacted by the Parliament, five years back, neither the state government not the central government has taken appropriate action for its implementation*".

The 1994 Act was both prohibitive and regulatory in nature. It imposed restrictions on the following.

6.5.1 Clinics, Medical Personnel and Sale of Machines

- Only registered genetic clinics can use pre-natal diagnostic techniques.
- By qualified medical practitioners.
- Prohibition of sex-selection.
- Prohibition on sale of ultrasound machine to unregistered laboratories, clinics and persons.

The essential elements of the Act are as follows:

Section 3A: Prohibition of Sex Selection: No person, including a specialist or a team of specialists in the field of infertility, shall conduct or cause to be conducted or aid in conducting by himself or by any other person, sex selection on a woman or a man or on both or on any tissue, embryo, conceptus, fluid, or gametes derived from either or both of them.

Section 3B: Prohibition on Sale of Ultrasound Machine, etc., to Persons, Laboratories, Clinics, etc., not Registered under this Act: No person shall sell any ultrasound machine or imaging machine or scanner or any other equipment capable of detecting sex of foetus to any genetic counselling centre, genetic clinic, and genetic laboratory or any other person not registered under this Act.

PNDT can be used for detection of abnormalities like:

- Chromosomal abnormalities.
- Genetic metabolic diseases.
- Haemoglobinopathies.
- Sex-linked genetic diseases.
- Congenital abnormalities.
- Any other abnormalities.

PNDT can be used under following conditions:

- Age of the pregnant women is above 35 years.
- Two or more spontaneous abortions.
- Pregnant women has been exposed to drugs, radiation, infection or chemicals.
- Family history of mental retardation or physical deformities.
- Any other condition.

Essential Communication:

- Explanation of all known side/after effects and test procedures.
- Written consent in a prescribed form.
- Not to disclose sex of the foetus by words, signs etc.
- Display prominently in local language that disclosure of sex of foetus is prohibited.
- Registration certificate to be displayed prominently in the clinic.

Regulatory Body:

- Policy making body—central and state supervisory board.
- Implementing body—state, district and then sub-district

appropriate authority.

- Advisory committee—state, district and then sub district advisory committee.

Husbands and Relatives:

- Cannot ask for pre-natal diagnostic techniques except for reasons permitted under the law.

Publishing and Advertising:

- Illegal—no person, organisation, counselling centre, laboratory is allowed.

Violation:

- Imprisonment of 3 years and ₹ 10,000 (₹ 50,000) fine, but subsequent conviction punishable with imprisonment for 5 years and ₹ 50,000 (₹ 1,00,000) fine.
- Offence to be cognizable, non-bailable and non-compoundable.

Implemented by Appropriate Authority

Role

- To grant, suspend or cancel registration.
- Enforce standards.
- Investigate complaints of breach of provisions.

Complaints

- Can be made by any person/social organisation.
- The chief medical officer to investigate.
- Can approach court if chief medical officer does not take action.
- Judicial magistrate first class or metropolitan magistrate.

6.5.2 Advisory Committee: The advisory committee shall consist of:

- Three medical experts including gynaecologists, obstetricians, paediatricians and medical geneticists.
- One legal expert.
- One officer to represent the department dealing with information and publicity of the State government.
- Three eminent social workers, at least one from the women's organisation.

The advisory committee may meet:

- as necessary.
- on the request of the appellate authority.
- for consideration of any application for registration and to give advice thereon; provided that the period intervening between any two meetings shall not exceed sixty days (Rule 15).

An application for registration shall be made to the appellate authority, in duplicate, in Form A, duly accompanied by an affidavit containing the relevant details.

An undertaking to the effect that the genetic counselling centre, genetic clinic and genetic laboratory shall not conduct any test procedure for selection of sex before or after conception or for detection of sex of foetus except for diseases specified in Section 4(2) nor shall the sex of foetus be disclosed to anybody.

An undertaking to the effect that the genetic counselling centre, genetic clinic, and genetic laboratory shall display prominently a notice that they do not conduct any techniques, tests or procedures, etc., by whatever name called, for detection of sex of foetus or for selection of sex before or after the conception.

The appropriate authority, or any person in his office authorized on this behalf, shall acknowledge receipt of the application for registration, in the acknowledgement slip provided at the bottom of Form A, immediately if delivered at the office of the appropriate authority, or not later than the next working day if received by post.

6.5.3 Certificate of Registration:

- The appropriate authority shall after holding an inquiry and after satisfying itself that the applicant has complied with all the requirements of this Act and the rules made there under and having regard to the advice of the advisory committee in this behalf, grant a certificate of registration in the prescribed form (Form B) jointly or separately to the G.C.C. /G.C./G.L., as the case may be.

- If after holding inquiry and after giving an opportunity of being heard to the applicant and having regard to the advice of the advisory committee, if the appropriate authority is satisfied that the applicant has not complied with the requirements of this Act or the rules, it shall, for the reasons to be recorded in writing, reject the application for registration and will be communicated to applicant in Form C.
- Every registration shall be renewed in such a manner and after such period and on payment of such fees as may be prescribed.
- The certificate of registration shall be displayed by the registered genetic counselling centre, genetic clinic, genetic laboratory, ultrasound clinic or imaging centre in a conspicuous place at its place of business.

6.5.4 Validity, Cancellation or Suspension of Registration

- Every certificate of registration shall be valid for a period of five years from the date of issue.
- The appropriate authority may suo moto, or on complaint, issue a notice to the genetic counselling centre, genetic clinic, genetic laboratory to show cause as to why its registration should not be cancelled or suspended for the reasons mentioned in the notice.
- If after giving a reasonable opportunity of being heard to the genetic counselling centre, genetic clinic, genetic laboratory and having regard to the advice of the advisory committee, the appropriate authority is satisfied that there has been a breach of the provisions of this Act or the rules, it may, without prejudice to any criminal action that it may take against such centre, laboratory, or clinic, suspend its registration for such period as it may think fit or cancel its registration, as the case may be.

Notwithstanding anything contained in above sub-section, if the appropriate authority is of the opinion that it is necessary or expedient to do so in the public interest, it may, for reason to be recorded in writing, suspend the registration of any genetic counselling centre, genetic clinic, genetic laboratory without issuing any such show cause notice.

6.5.5 Maintenance and Preservation of Records:

- Genetic counselling, genetic laboratory, genetic clinic or ultrasound clinic or imaging centre shall maintain a register showing, in serial order, the names and addresses of the men or women given genetic counselling, subjected to pre-natal diagnostic procedure or test, the name of their spouse or father and the date on which they first reported for such counselling or procedure of test.
- The record to be maintained by every genetic counselling centre, in respect of each women counselled, shall be specified in Form D.
- The record to be maintained by every genetic laboratory, in respect of each man or woman subjected to any pre-natal diagnostic procedure/technique/test, shall be as specified in Form E.
- The record to be maintained by every genetic clinic, in respect of each man or woman subjected to any pre-natal diagnostic procedure/technique/test, shall be as specified in Form F.
- The appropriate authority shall maintain a register, a permanent record of application for grant or renewal of certificate of registration as specified in Form H.
- Before conducting any pre-implantation genetic diagnosis, or any pre-natal diagnostic technique/test/procedure such as amniocentesis, chorionic villi biopsy, foetoscopy, foetal skin or organ biopsy or cordocentesis, a written consent, as specified in Form G in a language the person undergoing such procedure understands, shall be obtained from her/him.
- Person conducting ultrasonography on a pregnant woman shall keep a complete record thereof in the clinic in such a manner as may be prescribed and any deficiency or inaccuracy found therein shall amount to contravention of provisions of Section 5 or Section 6 unless the contrary is

proved by the person conducting such ultrasonography.

6.5.6 Intimation of Changes in Employees, Place or Equipment:

- Genetic laboratory/genetic clinic/genetic counselling centre shall intimate every change of employee, place, address and equipment installed, to the appropriate authority within a period of thirty days of such change (Rule 13).
- Public information (Rule 17).
- Prominent display of notice at its premises in English and in any other local language or language for the information of the public, to the effect that disclosure of sex of foetus is prohibited under law.
- At least one copy of the Act and the rule shall be available.
- The appellate authority and the state government may publish periodically, lists of registered centres and findings from the reports and other information in their possession, for the information of the public and for use by the experts in the field.

But there are various loopholes in the Act, which has made it a failure to a great extent, thus letting the demons of female foeticide, survive and flourish. Hence, the PNDT Act, 2002 was passed to plug the loopholes.

6.6 Pre-Natal Diagnostic Techniques (Regulation and Prevention of Misuse) Amendment Act, 2002

Objectives:

"The practices relating to female foeticide and techniques connected with the same are considered discriminatory to the female sex and not conducive to the dignity of women".

The new technologies for the determination of the sex are creating an imbalance in the male-female sex ratio. Hence, the state is duty bound to intervene in this matter for the welfare of the society. Therefore, the government felt the necessity to enact and implement a legislation to ban the pre-conception sex selection techniques and the misuse of pre-natal diagnostic techniques for sex selective abortions and to provide for the regulation of such abortions. Such a law is also needed to uphold medical ethics and initiate the process of regulation of medical technology in the larger interests cf the society.

Hence, it was proposed by the government to amend the aforesaid Act with a view to banning the use of both sex selection techniques prior to conception as well as misuse of pre-natal diagnostic techniques for sex selective abortions and to regulate such techniques with a view to ensure their scientific use for which they are intended.

6.6.1 Highlights:

- The Act provides for the prohibition and regulation of sex determination techniques before or after conception. [12]
- For the words and brackets, "the pre-natal diagnostic techniques (regulation and prevention of misuse)", the words and brackets "the pre-conception and pre-natal diagnostic techniques (prohibition of sex selection)" shall be substituted. [13] This lays a lot of emphasis on the issue of female foeticide in particular.
- Definitions of "conceptus", "embryo" and "foetus" have been laid down specifically that help in determining the cause and stage of PNDT.
- The explanation added to Section 2(ii) in clause d has enlarged the equipment machinery.
- Qualifications of geneticists have been upgraded. [14]
- Amendment of Section 17 of principal Act is as follows: *"To take appropriate legal action against the use of any sex selection technique by any person at any place, suo moto or brought to the notice and also to initiate independent investigations in such matter".*

This provision has given extra scope to the authorities for the utilization of the powers to fulfil their duties.

Insertion of a new Section 17A which reads as, "The appropriate authority shall have the powers in respect of the following matters, namely:

- summoning of any person who is in possession of any information relating to the violation of the provisions of this Act or rules made there under;

- production of any document or material object relating to clause (a);
- issuing search warrant for any place suspected to be indulging in sex selection techniques or pre-natal sex determination; and
- any other matter which may be prescribed.

This provision is very much tuned with the objective of Section 17(e):

- Provision with regard to the advertisements has been made more stringent. [15]
- Definitely the strongest provision of the bill is the new Section 24 which if brought to effect, shall epic out all doubts with regard to the application of penal provisions to women undergoing the PNDT tests. The provision has rightly identified the problems of women in the cases of PNDT as in most cases women are forced to go for these tests or to forgo their marital lives, their homes and even their lives. [16]

6.7 Indian Penal Code (I.P.C.), 1860

Relevant provisions of I.P.C. that deal with the problem of female foeticide are as follows.

6.7.1 Section 312—Causing Miscarriage: Whoever voluntarily causes a woman with child to miscarry, shall, if such miscarriage be not caused in good faith for the purpose of saving the life of the woman, be punished with imprisonment of either description for a term which may extend to three years, or with fine, or with both, and, if the woman be quick with child, shall be punished with imprisonment of either description for a term which may extend to seven years, and shall also be liable to fine.

Explanation: A woman who causes herself to miscarry, is within the meaning of this Section.

This Section requires two essentials, viz.:

- Voluntarily causing a woman to miscarry (abort), and

- Such miscarriage (abortion) should not have been caused in good faith for the purpose of saving the life of the woman.

The explanation clause appended to Section 312, I.P.C. makes it clear that the offender could be woman herself or any other person. As early as 1886, a woman [17] was charged for using herself to miscarry, though she had been pregnant for only one month, and there was nothing which could be called a foetus or a 'child'. The lower court acquitted the women taking a lenient view of the matter. But the High Court held the acquittal bad in law emphasising that it was the absolute duty of a prospective mother to protect her infant from the very moment of conception.

In *Queen Empress vs. Aruna Begum,* [18] where the term of pregnancy was almost complete and an attempted abortion resulted in the birth of the child, a conviction under Section 312 was set aside and one under Section 511, I.P.C., for attempt to bring about miscarriage was maintained.

The provision by implication recognizes the foetus right to life. [19] Section 312, I.P.C., permits abortion only on therapeutic (medical) grounds in order to protect the life of the mother.

In *Sharif vs. State of Orissa* [20], the Orissa High Court held that where termination of pregnancy of minor girl was performed to save the life of the mother, Section 312, I.P.C., is not attracted. In the impugned case, the accused accompanied the girl with her consent to nursing home, who wanted termination of pregnancy to avoid the social stigma. The accused did not instruct her to go for termination. Held, the accused is not liable for causing the girl to miscarry. [21]

6.7.2 Section 313—Causing Miscarriage without Woman's Consent: Whoever commits the offence defined in the last preceding Section without the consent of the woman, whether the woman is quick with child or not, shall be punished with [imprisonment for life] or with imprisonment of either description for a term which may extend to ten years, and shall also be liable to fine.

Sections 313 to 316 of the Indian Penal Code provide for enhanced punishment in cases of aggravating nature of the offence of miscarriage. Section 313, I.P.C., penalises voluntarily causing miscarriage of a woman with child without her consent, while miscarriage with consent is dealt with under Section 312, I.P.C. Under Section 313, I.P.C., only the person procuring the abortion is liable to punishment, whereas under Section 312, I.P.C., the woman is also liable to punishment. [22]

In *Moideenkutty Haji vs. Kunhikaya*, [23] the Kerala High Court held that an offence under Section 313, I.P.C., could not be made out, where the only allegation in the complaint was that on hearing that the woman was pregnant, the accused took her to a doctor, who terminated her pregnancy and there was no case that it was without her consent. On the contrary, the averment showed that the woman willingly submitted herself to abortion and even thereafter had sexual intercourse with the accused and there was nothing to show that abortion was at instance of the accused. Further, it was not clear from the allegation whether he was only accompanying the lady at her request and whether he even made a request to the doctor to have the abortion done. Finally, the doctor who conducted the abortion was not made an accused, which showed that she had no complaint against him.

6.7.3 Section 314—Death Caused by Act Done with Intent to Cause Miscarriage: Whoever, with intent to cause the miscarriage of woman with child, does any act which causes the death of such woman, shall be punished with imprisonment of either description for a term which may extend to ten years, and shall also be liable to fine.

If act done without woman's consent—and if the act is done without the consent of the woman, shall be punished either with [imprisonment for life] or with the punishment above mentioned.

Explanation: It is not essential to this offence that the offender should know that the act is likely to cause death.

6.7.4 Section 315—Act Done with Intent to Prevent Child Being Born Alive or to Cause it to Die after Birth: Whoever before the birth of any child does any act with the intention of thereby preventing the child from being born alive or causing it to die after its birth, and by such act prevent that child from being born alive, or causes it to die after its birth, shall, if such act be not caused in good faith for the purpose of saving the life of the mother, be punished with imprisonment of either description for a term which may extend to ten years, or with fine, or with both.

This Section is aimed at foeticide while in the womb after the foetus develops sufficiently to assume the human form which it does in normal cases in the sixth month. When it attains that degree of development the act which would, if done earlier, be abortion, ceases to be so as the delivery of an undeveloped child would be premature labour, for which the accused is held more responsible owing to mere advanced stage of foetal life.

In spite of claiming ourselves to be an ancient civilized and cultured society, it is found that even in many well educated and wealthy families, female child is not welcomed with open arms. Unfortunately, the new technology is being used to perpetuate gender bias. For example, in recent past pre-natal diagnostic centres have mushroomed throughout the country [24] which help in determining sex of the foetus that enable people to choose to abort female foetus. Indian parents still believe that having a daughter is like watering someone else's field.

The tentacles of pre-natal diagnostic centres are no more confined to urban areas and cities.

"Mobile killer clinics" have reached even to remote rural areas. These mobile clinics conduct sex-determination tests for sums ranging between ₹ 100 to ₹ 1,000 and earn huge money by resorting to illegal practices of getting girl child foetus aborted. [25] Resultantly, the number of infanticide cases in the country during 2005 increased by 5.9 percent.

In 2003, the apex Court in *Centre for Enquiry into Health and Allied Themes (CEHAT) vs. Union of India,* [26] expressing concern about the misuse of modern science and technology in preventing the birth of a girl child, directed the concerned authorities to strictly monitor the activities of the ultrasound diagnostic clinics to prevent illegal female foeticide. However, with no change in the mindset about females, the sex determination tests added to the adverse situation.

Unfortunately sex ratio keeps getting worse in India: it is shocking to note that in spite of the average figure of 927 girls for 1,000 boys, it puts India right at the bottom of the chart internationally. According to the report, only China with 832 girls per 1,000 boys ranks below India on this dubious front. [27]

6.7.5 Section 316—Causing Death of Quick Unborn Child by Act Amounting to Culpable Homicide: Whoever does any act under such circumstances, that if he thereby caused death, would be guilty of culpable homicide, and does by such act cause the death of a quick unborn child, shall be punished with imprisonment of either description for a term which may extend to ten years, and shall also be liable to fine.

Illustration: A, knowing that he is likely to cause the death of a pregnant woman, does an act which, if it caused the death of the woman, would amount to culpable homicide. The woman is injured, but does not die, but the death of an unborn quick child with which she is pregnant is thereby caused. A is guilty of the offence defined in this Section.

Ingredients:

- The woman was quick with child;
- The accused did an act to cause the death of the child.
- The circumstances under which the act was done were such as to make the accused guilty of culpable homicide if death has been caused.

In *Pappan vs. State* [28] the accused gave two fatal blows to his wife, who was in an advanced stage of pregnancy. She succumbed to her injuries within 24 hours. It caused death of her quick unborn child also. Accused was prosecuted and convicted for offences punishable under Sections 304 and 316. In an appeal, the High Court found him guilty for the offence of murder of his wife punishable under Section 302 but acquitted him of the charge under Section 316 holding that Section 316 has no application to a case where act attributed to accused has resulted in the death of a pregnant woman.

Endnotes

1. 410 U.S. 113 (1973).
2. The U.S. Supreme Court in two landmark decisions, *Roe vs. Wade*, 41 USLW 4213 (1973) and *Deo vs. Bolton*, 41 USLW 4233 (1973), upheld the right of woman to an abortion for the first three months of pregnancy as being an element in the right of privacy given by the Fourteenth Amendment to the US Constitution.
3. *H.L. vs. Matheson*, 450 US 398 (1980).
4. Gazette of India, 17th November 1969, Part II, Section 2, page 880 for Statement of Objects and Reasons of the Medical Termination of Pregnancy Bill, 1969.
5. (1) Notwithstanding anything contained in the Indian Penal Code, a registered medical practitioner shall not be guilty of any offence under that Code or any other law for the time being in force, if any pregnancy is terminated by him in accordance with the provisions of this Act. (2) Subject to the provisions of sub-section 4, a pregnancy may be terminated by a registered medical practitioner: (a) where the length of the pregnancy does not exceed twelve weeks, if such medical practitioner is, or (b) where the length of pregnancy exceeds twelve weeks but does not exceed twenty weeks, if not less than two registered medical practitioners are, of opinion, formed in good faith: (i) the continuance of the pregnancy would involve a risk to the life of the pregnancy woman or of grave injury to her physical or mental health; or (ii) there is a substantial risk that if the child is born, it would suffer from such physical or mental abnormalities as to be seriously handicapped.
6. (1994) 3 SCC 430.
7. http://symlaw.spiggi.com/wp-content/uploads/2006/08/pndt_report.pdf.
8. http://symlaw.spiggi.com/wp-

content/uploads/2006/08/pndt_report.pdf.

9. *A.K. Gopalan vs. State of Madras*, 1950 AIR 27.
10. Sourced and modified from Amar Jesani and Aditi Iyers, "Abortion: Who is Responsible for Our Rights", google.com, Last visited on 13th November, 2012.
11. *Centre for Inquiry into Health and Allied Themes vs. UOI*; (2001) 5 SCC 579.
12. The long title of the bill that is proposed to be substituted for present long title reads as follows: In the Pre-Natal Diagnostic Techniques (Regulation and Prevention of Misuse) Act,1994 (hereinafter referred to as the principal act), for the long title, the following long title shall be substituted, namely, "An Act to provide for the prohibition of sex selection, before or after conception, and for regulation of pre-natal diagnostic techniques for the purposes of detecting genetic abnormalities or metabolic disorders or chromosomal abnormalities or certain congenital malformations or sex-linked disorders and for the prevention of their misuse for sex determination leading to female foeticide and for matters connected therewith or incidental thereto".
13. Amendment of Section 1 of the Act.
14. Definition of (g) of the Act, 2002.
15. Substitution of new section for Section 22. For Section 22 of the Principal Act, the following section shall be substituted, namely: (1) No person, organization, genetic counselling centre, genetic laboratory or genetic clinic, including clinic, laboratory or centre having ultrasound machine or imaging machine or scanner or any other technology capable of undertaking determination of sex of foetus or sex selection shall issue, publish, distribute, communicate or cause to be issued, published, distributed or communicated any advertisement, in any form, including internet, regarding facilities of pre-natal determination of sex or sex selection before conception available at such centre, laboratory, clinic or at any other place. (2) No person or organization including genetic counselling centre, genetic laboratory or genetic clinic shall issue, publish, distribute, communicate or cause to be issued, published, distributed or communicated any advertisement in any manner regarding pre-natal determination or preconception selection of sex by any means whatsoever, scientific or otherwise. (3) Any person who contravenes the provisions of sub-section (1) or sub-section (2)

shall be punishable with imprisonment for a term which may extend to three years and with fine which may extend to ten thousand rupees.

16. Section 24...Notwithstanding anything contained in the Indian Evidence Act, 1872, the court shall presume unless the contrary is proved that the pregnant woman was compelled by her husband or any other relative, as the case may be, to undergo pre-natal diagnostic technique for the purposes other than those specified in sub-section (2) of Section 4 and such person shall be liable for abetment of offence under sub-section (3) of Section 23 and shall be punishable for the offence specified under that section.
17. *Q.E. vs. Ademma*, 1886 ILR 9 Mad 369.
18. (1873) 19 WR (Cr) 230.
19. Bonda, "The Impact of Constitutional Law on the Protection of Urban Human Life: Some Comparative Remarks", *Human Rights* (1977), pp. 233-235.
20. 1996 Cr LJ 2826 (Ori.).
21. K.D. Gaur, "Criminal Law and Materials", 3rd Edition, 1999, pp. 464-470.
22. *Queen Empress vs. Aruna Begum*, (1873) 19 WR (Cr) 230.
23. A.I.R. 1987 Ker 184 (FB).
24. In a small town like Palwal (in Rajasthan) there are reportedly over 150 ultrasound clinics particularly with the purpose of determining sex of the child, *Times of India*, May 14, 2001, p. 10.
25. See Seethlakshmi S., Times News Network, *Times of India*, 8th November, 2002, Lucknow edition, p. 7.
26. 2003 (7) SCALE 345: AIR 2003 SC 3309.
27. *Times of India*, 8th September, 2007, Pune edition, p. 13.
28. A.I.R. 1966 All. 590.

7

Judicial Activism to Eradicate Female Foeticide

Today, the Supreme Court of India has become a champion of every cause in the Indian society. It is a guardian and guarantor of every human being, whether living or yet to be born. In order to check rampant practice of killing of female foetus, it has issued a warning to all concerned authorities. To check female foeticide, the Pre-Natal Diagnostic Techniques (Regulation and Prevention of Misuse) Act, 1994 was enacted.

The Act came into force in 1996. By itself, it is a comprehensive legislation which lays down the conditions in which the use of pre-natal diagnostic techniques is prohibited as also where it is regulated. It has provisions for establishing mechanisms responsible for policy making under the Act and also those responsible for the implementation of the Act. The penalties for various offences are also elaborated.

During the course of the implementation of this Act, certain inadequacies and practical difficulties in its administration came to the Government's notice. At the same time, newer techniques have been developed to select the sex of the child even before conception leading to a further decline in the sex ratio. These developments were also taken note of by the Supreme Court in its various orders in a public interest litigation filed by an NGO, *CEHAT and Others vs. Union of India and Others*. The Court had laid down the amendments to the PNDT Act and the amended Act came into force from February 14, 2003. Its main purpose has been to ban the use of sex-selection techniques before or after conception as well as the misuse of pre-natal diagnostic techniques for sex-selective abortions and to regulate such techniques. The implementation of the Act rests with the States and Union Territories.

As a part of the implementation of the Act, appropriate authorities are constituted and each is assisted by an eight member advisory committee. The committee consists of doctors, lawyers, social workers, and officers dealing with the media. Supervisory boards have also been constituted under the chairpersonship of the Minister of Health and Family Welfare to oversee the implementation of the Act. [1]

As per the reports received from States/UTs, more than 21,600 centres conducting pre-natal diagnostic procedure including ultra-sonography have been registered under the PC and PNDT Act. So far more than 400 complaints have been filed in various courts for violation of the Act and rules.

7.1 Landmark Judgements

The Indian courts have tried interpreting the law in many cases and some of the landmark judgements are as follows.

In *Centre for Enquiry into Health and Allied Themes (CEHAT) and Others* [2], a public interest litigation was filed under Article 32 of the Constitution of India, by Centre for Enquiry into Health and Allied Themes (CEHAT), a research organisation; Mahila Sarvangin Utkarsh Mandal (MASUM), a non-governmental organization and Dr. Sabu M. George, a civil society member. In this petition, it took nearly one year for various States to file their affidavits in reply/written submissions and after hearing them, from time to time, the Supreme Court has issued a number of directions to the Central and State Governments, to the Central Supervisory Board and appropriate authorities established under the Act, for its proper implementation with all vigour and zeal.

The first set of directions were issued on May 4, 2001 whereby both State and Central Governments were directed to create public awareness against the practice of pre-natal sex determination and sex selection and to implement the Act in the earnest interest. Central Supervisory Board was directed to review and monitor the implementation of the Act and at the same time to examine the necessity to amend the Act in view of the emerging technology of pre-conception sex selection and difficulties encountered in implementation of the Act. State Governments were directed to immediately appoint fully empowered appropriate authorities and appropriate authorities were further directed to take appropriate criminal action in case of violation of the provisions of the Act. Being aware of the lackadaisical manner in which the Governments were functioning, the Supreme Court did not stop merely by issuing directions but called for the compliance reports and kept the matter pending for further directions on August 6, 2001.

In spite of these directions by the Supreme Court—as certain States did not file compliance affidavits—the matter had to be adjourned from time to time and on September 19, 2001, the Supreme Court recorded with anguish that directions were not complied with and there was a total disregard on the part of administration in implementation of the Act. The Supreme Court issued further directions for taking appropriate criminal action against the medical officers and the clinics violating the provisions of the Act.

On November 7, 2001, in the same writ petition, on the suggestion of Central Government, the Supreme Court ordered setting up of National Inspection and Monitoring Committee for the implementation of the Act. In the year 2003, in conformity with the several directions issued by the Supreme Court, the Act was amended to bring within its purview, the misuse of pre-conception and pre-natal diagnostic techniques and was titled as the Pre-conception and Pre-natal Diagnostic Techniques (Prohibition of Sex Selection) Act. On March 31, 2003 and September 10, 2003, after giving some further directions, for creating public awareness and for effective implementation of the amended Act, the Supreme Court finally disposed of the petition on September 10, 2003.

The perusal of these directions in the form of six orders is sufficient to reflect that the Supreme Court has, in this matter, literally legislated on how the Act should be implemented. This decision hence constitutes a landmark in its impact. It exhibits the deep concern and the anguish felt by the Apex Court towards the social evil of sex selection followed by elimination of foetus if found to be female. The Supreme Court was equally concerned with the apathy on the part of Government in implementation of the law which aims at preventing such a social evil. As per the Supreme Court, "it was unfortunate that for implementation of the law, which was the urgent need of the hour, NGOs had to approach the Court". The significance given by the Supreme Court to this issue is bound to have a positive effect for advancing the cause.

As the judgments and orders of Supreme Court are binding on all in view of Article 141 of the Constitution of India and as the non-obedience and non-compliance with the directions issued by the Supreme Court amounts to contempt of court, it appears that only with a view to avoid facing the action of contempt of the Supreme Court, the Government and the authorities have at least made some efforts towards the implementation of this Act. This decision in that respect is epoch making.

It must be stated that, but for the initiative taken by the NGOs and the constant monitoring by the Apex Court, virtually laying down the entire framework for implementation, this Act would have remained on paper only.

There were six orders that were passed by the Apex Court in this writ petition and are worth reading in entirety, especially the opening paras of the Supreme Court's first order dated May 4, 2001 and last order dated September 10, 2003, highlighting the plight of female child and the inhuman practice of sex selection. The Supreme Court had laid down directions for central and state governments, central supervisory body and other appropriate authorities.

In *Vinod Soni and Others vs. Union of India,* [3] the validity of the Act was challenged on the ground that the provisions of the Act are violative of Article 21 of the Constitution of India. A very interesting argument was advanced in this case by the petitioner that the right to life guaranteed under Article 21 of the Constitution includes right to personal liberty which in turns includes the liberty of choosing the sex of the offspring and to determine the nature of the family. Therefore, it was contended that the couple is entitled to undertake any such medical procedure which provides for determination or selection of sex.

The High Court however exposed the fallacy of this argument by observing that, "right to personal liberty cannot be expanded by any stretch of imagination to liberty to prohibit to coming into existence of a female or male foetus which shall be for the nature to decide". After making reference to the decisions of the Supreme Court, which explain that Article 21 includes the right to food, clothing, decent environment and even protection of cultural heritage, the High Court held that "these rights, even if, further expanded to the extremes of the possible elasticity of the provisions of Article 21, cannot include right to selection of sex, whether pre-conception or post-conception". It was observed by the High Court that "this Act is factually enacted to further the right of the child to full development as given under Article 21. A child conceived is, therefore, entitled under Article 21 to full development, whatever be the sex of that child". Accordingly, the High Court dismissed the petition by holding that it does not even make a prima facie case for violation of Article 21 of the Constitution (Para 8).

The case leaves one wondering how right to life of a person can be expanded to include selection of sex of the child.

In Vijay Sharma and others vs. Union of India [4], a writ petition was filed under Article 226 of the Constitution of India, by one Mr. Vijay Sharma and others and the validity of the Act was challenged on the ground that it violates principle of 'equality of law' enshrined in Article 14 of the Constitution of India. The petitioners were a married couple having two female children and were desirous of having a male child. According to them, by doing so, they could then enjoy the love and affection of both son and daughter and their daughters can enjoy the company of their own brother while growing up.

According to them, couples who are already having children of one sex should be allowed to make use of the pre-natal diagnostic techniques at pre-conception stage to have the child of opposite sex. It was further argued that under the provisions of the Medical Termination of Pregnancy Act, 1972 (MTP Act), termination of pregnancy is allowed under certain circumstances, hence there is no reason to impose a blanket ban on determination of sex at pre-conception stage. An innovative plea was raised to the effect that, if anguish caused by unwanted pregnancy is recognized as a ground for the termination of the pregnancy under MTP Act, why under PC and PNDT Act, anguish caused to a mother who conceives a female or male child for the second or third time is not considered and thus there is discrimination between two women placed in similar positions and hence the Act violates Article 14 of the Constitution.

The honourable judges of the High Court, after elaborately dealing with the object, reasons and provisions of the Act, held that there can be no comparison between the two legislations viz., the MTP Act and the PCPNDT Act. The objects of both the Acts differ. MTP Act does not deal with sex selection before or after conception. Anguish of a mother who does not want to bear a child of a particular sex cannot be equated with a mother who wants to terminate the pregnancy not because of the sex of child but for other circumstances. Thus, by process of comparative study, the High Court held that provisions of the Act cannot be called as discriminatory and hence violative of Article 14 of the Constitution.

The High Court had in this case taken note of the frightening figure showing imbalance in sex ratio in various parts of India and expressed its concern for the same. The High Court was also aghast at the shocking arguments in the petition proclaiming that if the country is economically and socially backward, it is better that female children are not born. The court has, in its strong and harsh words held that, "such tendency affects the dignity of women. It undermines their importance. It insults and humiliates womanhood. It violates woman's right to life. Sex selection, is therefore, against the spirit of the law and the Constitution". Thus, rejecting all the challenges raised as regards the Constitutional validity of the Act, the court dismissed the petition and directed the State to take all expeditious steps to prevent misuse of the diagnostic techniques.

The entire judgment of the High Court must be read from start to finish. It makes out a strong case for upholding the validity of the Act.

In *Malpani Infertility Clinic Pvt. Ltd. and Others vs. Appropriate Authority PNDT Act and Others* [5], a writ petition was filed by M/s Malpani Infertility Clinic Pvt. Ltd. in the High Court of Bombay and the order passed by the appropriate authority suspending the registration of petitioner's diagnostic centre under the PNDT Act was challenged. Main contention raised was that a show cause notice, as contemplated under Section 20(1), an opportunity of hearing as contemplated under Section 20(2) and sufficient reasons as required under Section 20(3) of the Act, were not given to the petitioners before taking the action of suspending registration; hence the order was bad as per the law.

However, considering peculiar facts of the case, the High Court rejected this contention. The petitioner's diagnostic centre was allegedly carrying out prohibited activities involving pre-natal sex determination, leading to female foeticide. Prima facie, there was some material before the authority, a prosecution lodged on the basis of which the authority had adequate power under the Act to suspend the licence pending prosecution. It cannot be said that there was no sufficient mention of reasons for authority to take action. It was held that, as the appropriate authority has, after referring to that criminal prosecution, issued the order of suspension, there was sufficient notice to petitioners and there was also sufficient mention of the reasons by the appropriate authority in suspension order.

It was further held that, "when the reasons are required to be given in writing, it is not necessary that there ought to be a detailed discussion". As regards the contention that Section 20(3) provides only for cancellation and not for suspension of the registration, it was pointed out that such power has to be read into the Section, otherwise the provisions of a welfare enactment will be rendered nugatory. In the words of High Court, "where there is a conflict of private interest, to carry on a particular activity which the public authority considered as damaging to the social interest, surely the power under the Statute has to be read as an enabling power".

In *Suo Moto vs. State of Gujarat* [6], the full bench decision of Gujarat High Court is a path breaking decision, wherein the Court has taken a progressive view in tune with the provisions of the Act. In this case, the full bench of the Gujarat High Court was deciding the reference made by single judge in the case of *Hitesh D. Shah vs. State of Gujarat* on several important legal issues, namely, whether the provisions of the proviso to sub-section (3) of Section 4 of the Act require that the complaint should contain specific allegation regarding the contravention of the provisions of Sections 5 and 6 of the Act; whether the burden lies on the authorities to prove that there was contravention of the provisions of Section 5 or 6 of the Act and whether any deficiency or inaccuracy in filing Form F, as required under the statuary provisions is merely a procedural lapse?

The genesis of the reference was the decision of single bench in the case of *Dr. Manish C. Dave vs. State of Gujarat*. [7] By this decision, a bunch of petitions for quashing criminal complaints filed against petitioners for the offence punishable under Sections 4 and 5 of the Act were allowed. The petitioners were radiologists using sonography machine for the purpose of diagnosis. The only allegation made against them was that they have failed to fill up Form F as required under Section 4(3) of the Act, which according to the prosecution, amounted to contravention of the provisions of Sections 5 and 6 of the Act.

However, in the absence of any specific allegation in the complaint that petitioners had conducted the tests for sex determination or communicated the sex of the foetus to any one, it was held by the single bench that deficiency in filling up Form F does not amount to contravention of the provisions of Sections 5 and 6 of the Act. Accordingly, it was further held that complaints themselves were not maintainable.

This observation made by High Court in the case of Manish C. Dave that "deficiency or inaccuracy in filling up of Form F is merely a procedural lapse which does not in any manner amount to contravention of the provisions of Sections 5 and 6 of the Act" was bound to prove fatal to prosecution, leading to setting aside of several such criminal cases.

Accordingly, in this reference, while answering these legal issues, it was held by the full bench that the rules are made and the forms are prescribed in aid of implementation of the Act to plug the possible loopholes in strict compliance of the Act and hence they are very important for implementation of the Act and for the prosecution of the offender that any improper maintenance of such record is itself made by the Act equivalent to violation of the proviso of Sections 5 and 6 by virtue of the proviso to sub-section (3) of Section 4 of the Act.

It was further held that improper maintenance of records also has consequences other than prosecution for the deemed violation of Section 5 or 6 because Section 20 provides for cancellation or suspension of registration of genetic counselling centre, genetic laboratory or genetic clinic in case of breach of the provisions of the Act or the rules framed there under. It was held that by virtue of the deeming provision of the proviso to sub-section (3) of Section 4, contravention of the provisions of Section 5 or 6 is to be legally presumed.

Hence, proviso to sub-section (3) of Section 4 of the Act does not require that the complaint alleging the inaccuracy or deficiency in maintaining record in the prescribed manner should also contain allegation of contravention of the provisions of Section 5 or 6 of the Act. It was further held that the burden to prove that there was contravention of these provisions does not lie upon the prosecution. It was accordingly held that, deficiency or inaccuracy in filling Form F as prescribed under Rule 9 of the rules made under the PNDT Act, being a deficiency or inaccuracy in keeping record in the prescribed manner, is not a procedural lapse but an independent offence amounting to contravention of the provisions of Section 5 or 6 of the PNDT Act and has to be treated and tried accordingly.

This judgement of full bench is really welcome because of the progressive interpretation given to these provisions. Otherwise the provisions of Section 4(3) of the Act would have been illusory or nugatory. This judgment is important in more than one area as it has held that not only the appropriate authority but any officer on whom the powers are conferred by the Central Government, the State Government or the appropriate authority itself can institute a complaint under the provisions of the Act and court can take cognizance on a compliant made by any officer authorized on that behalf. Thus, in this case, the Court has widened the scope of the term 'appropriate authority and recognized the locus standi of any officer authorized by such appropriate authority to file complaint and set the law in motion in case of violation of the provisions of the Act.

In Chitra Agrwal (Dr.) vs. State of Uttaranchal [8], the petitioner was a practising doctor having an ultrasound centre registered under the PNDT Act, 1994. The facts of this petition are to the effect that the registration of the petitioner's ultrasound/sonography centre was first suspended and then cancelled. The petitioner filed an appeal before the State Appellate Authority, challenging the cancellation of the registration. However, the appellate authority informed the petitioner that the appeal cannot be entertained as the criminal proceedings initiated against the petitioner were pending before the High Court. The petitioner therefore approached the High Court under Article 226 of the Constitution challenging the cancellation of the registration.

The High Court found that the State Appellate Authority was not right in not entertaining the appeal of the petitioner simply on the ground that criminal proceedings in respect of the same incident were pending against the petitioner. The High Court explained in detail, the difference between the two. It was held that the action of cancellation of registration is directed against the ultrasound centre and not against the owner of the centre; whereas criminal action is directed against the person who has committed the offence under the Act. Both the actions are independent and they can be dealt with simultaneously. The pendency of criminal proceedings need not and should not deter the appellate authority from deciding the appeal filed against the cancellation of registration. Accordingly, the High Court directed the State Appellate Authority to take appropriate decision in accordance with the law, as early as possible and at any date within a period of 3 weeks.

This judgment thus provides guidance to State Appropriate Authorities when to entertain or not to entertain the appeal, when simultaneously several actions are being initiated. The judgment also explains the difference between the penal action and the action of suspension and cancellation of registration.

In *Pradeep Ohri vs. State of Punjab and Others* [9], the petitioner was convicted under Section 23(1) of the Act and was released on probation by the trial court. Initially, he was legally advised that it was not necessary for him to file appeal against the conviction. However, subsequently as per the legal advice, he preferred an appeal along with an application for condonation of delay. Meanwhile, after more than one year of his conviction by the trial court, the Petitioner's name was removed from the State Medical Register by the Medical Council under Section 23(2) of the Act. By this writ petition, he has challenged this order for removal of his name.

The first contention raised was that his name was removed from the State Medical Register for a period of 5 years for an offence committed on July 9, 2002 when as per Section 23 of the old PNDT Act, 1994, his name could have been removed only for a period 2 years. It was submitted that only after the amendment of the PNDT Act with effect from February 14, 2003, the period of 2 years for the first offence had been enhanced to 5 years. Therefore, it was argued that the order of removal of his name for 5 years in respect of the act committed prior to the new amended Act came into effect, was squarely hit by the Constitutional prohibition as imposed by Article 20(1) of the Constitution against retrospective effect to any penal law. The High Court accepted and upheld the said contention and reduced the period to 2 years from 5 years.

The second contention raised was that as the petitioner was not sentenced to any punishment but was released on probation, no disqualification was attached to his conviction. Hence, the Medical Council had acted illegally and without jurisdiction while ordering the removal of his name. It was submitted that this order was grossly in violation of Section 12 of the Probation of Offenders Act. The High Court however rejected the said contention and confirmed the removal of his name for two years.

In *State through District Appropriate Authority cum Civil Surgeon, Faridabad vs. Dr. Anil Sabhani and Others* [10], the court held that the PCPNDT Act is a recent piece of legislation. Further, as observed by the Apex Court and various High Courts, there has been total inaction, apathy and lack of interest on the part of the Government in implementing the provisions of the Act. Hence, there are very few cases registered for violating the provisions of the Act. Out of these also, very few have reached a logical conclusion, even at the trial stage.

The below mentioned case is one of the first of its kind cases, in which conviction for violation of various provisions and the rules under the Act was recorded and it was followed by a deterrent punishment.

This case was registered on the complaint of the District Appropriate Authority cum Civil Surgeon, Faridabad. On the basis of three decoy patients sent to the ultrasound centre of the accused, it was established that accused No. 1 and 2 were indulging in the illegal act of sex determination and violating the provisions of the Act and the rules framed hereunder. Hence, with the help of the task force and three pregnant women acting as decoy patients, namely Mrs. Santosh, Mrs. Raveeta and Mrs. Madhu, a sting operation was conducted at the ultrasound centre and accused No. 1 and 2 were nabbed red handed while performing ultrasonography on a pregnant women and disclosing the sex of the foetus. The marked currency notes and the record of ultrasonography test were seized from their possession.

Both the accused had admitted in their handwriting that they had charged ₹ 300 plus ₹ 1,200 for sex determination of Mrs. Madhu and had only made entry of ₹ 300. They had further admitted in writing about the non-issuance of any receipt of cash to the patient Mrs. Madhu and of accepting the money for conveying sex of the foetus to her. Both the accused were therefore taken into custody and charged for contravening provisions of Sections 6(a) and 6(b) of the Act. When a sting operation was conducted at their clinic, it was found that the accused were conducting PNDT procedures in violation of Sections 5(1) and 5(2) of the Act and using ultrasound for revealing sex of the unborn foetus in violation of Sections 4(1), 4(2) and 4(3) of the Act and also failing to maintain proper records of the ultrasound centre and contravening the provisions of Section 29 read with Rule 9 and Form F under PNDT Act rules and all the offences punishable under Section 23 of the Act.

As both the accused pleaded not guilty, prosecution examined 9 witnesses and proved the incident of sending decoy patients for examination and of conducting the raid by the task force. Prosecution also relied upon various documentary evidences. In defence, the accused examined 3 witnesses namely, decoy patients Mrs. Madhu, Mrs. Santosh and Santosh's husband Mr. Sohan Pal. All of them disowned the statements recorded by the appropriate authority and denied the occurrence of any such incident. Several contentions were raised by the accused to challenge the prosecution case, which were dealt with by the court one by one and with sound reasoning, they were rejected. The Court found both the accused guilty for commission of all the offences alleged against them and sentenced them to undergo simple imprisonment for 2 years and to pay fine of ₹ 5,000 each and in case of default, a further imprisonment of 3 months.

In the entire judgment, the Court has consciously placed emphasis upon the object and reasons of the Act, the circumstances under which it was brought into existence and expressed concern for the continuously declining sex ratio due to the rampant misuse of scientific diagnostic techniques. What was more important was that the Court did not stop merely at expressing its concern but also handled the case in a very pragmatic and sensitive manner while appreciating the evidence. In the end, the Court by condemning the acts of the accused, imposed deterrent punishment on the accused so that no one indulges in such a heinous crime.

While appreciating the evidence on record the Court has, being aware of the different and typical nature of the case ignored minor contradictions pointed out by defence counsel in the statements of witnesses. The defence tried to cash in on the fact that there were inconsistencies in the evidence of prosecution witnesses with respect to the presence of appropriate authority along with the team conducting the sting operation. The Court held that the said fact was not of much importance as the appropriate authority was not the sole witness on which the case is based and hence it does not affect the merits of the case.

The Court also rejected the defence argument about absence of any written complaint against accused, by observing that when there were several oral complaints against the accused of violating the provisions of the Act, appropriate authority was not required to wait for the written complaint and then to take action; on the contrary, the appropriate authority was bound, competent and was correct in investigating the oral complaints also.

The Court then placed reliance on the statements of the

accused recorded by the appropriate authority at the time of the sting operation. As per the defence counsel, appropriate authority had no right to obtain such statements and the said statements being confessional in nature, cannot be used against the accused. However, observing that these statements are in the handwriting of accused and were contemporaneous and corroborative piece of circumstantial evidence, the Court relied upon them to prove the guilt of the accused.

The Court rejected the defence argument about non-joining of independent witnesses from the place at which the sting operation was conducted, by holding that it was not very material in the present case as the team had earlier taken precaution of including in its team, Dr. Mini Vora who was not a doctor working for Government, but in fact a private doctor and was the Secretary of the Indian Medical Association, Faridabad.

The Court also appreciated the efforts taken by the prosecution team in bringing the accused to the book although the case was first of its kind, registered way back in 2001, and the appropriate authority had never played the role of an investigating agency like police. Even then they had completed the investigation to the best of their knowledge and capability.

At the same time, the Court has also brought to notice that, the appropriate authority and its team, who had done a lot of hard work in preparation and subsequent sting at the clinic of the accused, did not show the same zeal at the time of conducting the trial. One of the reasons for the Court to make such an observation was that no necessary steps were taken by the prosecution to prove the evidence of conversation between the accused, Mrs. Madhu, the witness and doctor Keval Kumar inside the clinic which was recorded on a tape though it was an important piece of evidence and would have added weightage to the prosecution case. Secondly, though the witness list of prosecution was of 18 witnesses, the prosecution was able to examine only 9 witnesses despite sufficient opportunity being granted by the Court and despite the fact that the presence of some more witnesses would have further helped the prosecution.

The best part of the judgment was the appreciation of the evidence of 3 defence witnesses, who were initially the witnesses for prosecution but at the time of trial, were examined by the accused as their witnesses. This appreciation of evidence was done in a proper and sensitive manner. The Court understood and put on record the circumstances under which these 3 witnesses came to depose in favour of the defence instead of the prosecution. The evidence of the two defence witnesses namely, Mrs. Santosh and Mrs. Madhu was very vital for prosecution as they were decoy patients and were also present at the time of the sting operation. However, in evidence, they denied everything and stated that they were induced by the task force members to accompany them and to raise a false alarm.

Their becoming hostile was fatal to the prosecution case. However, only because of proper appreciation of their evidence, prosecution could get over this obstacle in reaching to conviction of the accused who had made every effort to escape from the clutches of law, even to the extent of winning over crucial prosecution witnesses.

The Court has in this respect brought to the notice of the prosecution the need to take care of such witnesses who by going against all odds tried to help prosecution with its case but then they were not cared for by the prosecution and hence became an easy prey for the accused to use them as their witnesses instead of the witnesses of the task force members.

In a nutshell, this judgment excels in all respects and is a major victory for the prosecution. It shows that if there is genuine interest and hard work, accompanied with sincere efforts, the laudable object of the Act can be achieved with success.

7.2 Shortcomings and Loopholes in the Law

The High Court has expressed serious concerns over the non-effective implementation of the law to prevent pre-natal sex determination tests; the Delhi High Court has suggested that the Central government plug the loopholes in the legislation.

"The absence of clear rules and guidelines spelling out unambiguously the qualification, training and experience required for operating a diagnostic clinic offering ultrasound tests, has resulted in unethical practices...going unchecked", noted Justice S. Muralidhar in his order.

The court said the Pre-Conception and Pre-Natal Diagnostic Techniques (Prohibition of Sex Selection) Act (PNDT Act) should be amended and asked the authorities to conduct a comprehensive survey after consulting the experts in the medical fraternity and education. As a result of the ambiguity in defining the term 'sonologist' under the PNDT Act, the growth of diagnostic clinics could not be effectively regulated, the court observed.

"The requirements in terms of qualification, training and experience to recognise and register as sonologist should be incorporated...In determining the criteria, the best available international practices should be adopted".

The shortcomings of the PNDT Act (2003) lie in criteria set for establishing a genetic counselling centre, genetic laboratory and genetic clinic/ultrasound clinic/imaging centre and person qualified to perform the tests.

- The terms genetic clinic/ultrasound clinic/imaging centre cannot be used interchangeably. But the Act does.
- Moreover, the amended Act should have categorically defined persons, laboratories, hospitals, institutions involved in pre-conception sex selective techniques such as artificial reproductive techniques and pre-implantation genetic diagnosis.
- Who is a qualified medical geneticist? As per the Act, "a person who possesses a degree or diploma or certificate in medical genetics in the field of PNDT or has a minimum 2 years experience after obtaining any medical qualification under the MCI Act, 1956 or a P.G. in biological sciences".

Many medical experts feel that a degree or diploma or 2 years experience in medical genetics cannot be made synonymous. [11]

- As per the Act, an ultrasound machine falls under the requirement of a genetic clinic, while it is widely used also by the hospitals and nursing homes not conducting pre-implantation genetic diagnosis (PGD) and PNDT.

Effective implementation of PC and PNDT needs to be assured through, ensuring registration, curbing the spread of mobile ultrasound, regulating sale of new machines, ensuring compliance of the Act like keeping records and submitting them to the authorities on time—preferably online—like the birth records are being done now, monitoring the functioning of these ultrasound clinics and complete audit of all pregnancy ultrasounds across the country (audit of all F forms submitted).

Another problem is that the appropriate authorities do not know their functions and responsibilities. Appropriate authorities do not have the necessary expertise and experience in legal matters. Deputing of medical professionals, or regulatory bodies under the PNDT Act, has not been an effective way to check the practice of sex determination, as doctors tend to be reluctant to book their fellow doctors.

The judiciary has tried to bring clarity in law by interpreting the PNDT Act in various ways through many of its landmark judgements but the problem has not been curbed due to various loopholes in the law. There is a serious need for amendment in the law because what was made to favour the women is indeed going against them as per the recent statistical data. Apart from the efforts made by the legislature and the judiciary, society along with the press, should work in coordination to make people aware of this problem and devise ways to bring this problem to an end.

7.3 National Legal Research Desk (NLRD)

The Constitution of India provides for special treatment of women, guarantees equality and prohibits discrimination. The

Government of India has been strengthening various laws focused on women and children. This has been more visible since the Beijing CEDAW Conference. The recent years have been witness to some landmark interpretations and directives related to violence against women. Despite the Constitutional mandate of equal legal status for men and women, the same is yet to be realized. The dejure laws have not been translated into de facto situation for various reasons such as illiteracy, social practices, prejudices, cultural norms based on patriarchal values, poor representation of women in policy-making, poverty, regional disparity in development, lack of access and opportunity to information and resources, etc. The ground situation more or less remains the same.

Most of the laws come with various institutional machineries, partnership between various stakeholders and active role of NGOs. These institutions need to be in existence in order for the law to be effective. Also the policies and programmes made at the top takes a long time to percolate to the bottom and there is an urgent need of sharing information and resources.

The awareness on laws and access to justice remains dismal. At the district and the state level, sensitivity on women rights among judicial officers, administration and the police is very low. This leads to a situation where the implementation of the law becomes difficult. Recently, India has increased its budgetary support for the implementation of various laws on violence against women and it becomes increasingly more important for the organization like *Shakti Vahini* to work on governance, specially related to women and children issues.

The National Legal Research Desk (NLRD) has been instituted to strengthen the implementation of the laws related to women and children in India. NLRD focuses on documenting the recent changes in the law, collect and compile the recent landmark judgments of the Supreme Court of India and the High Courts and ensure a wider dissemination of the same through the government and the non-government machinery. The NLRD will work with law enforcement agencies, police academies, judicial agencies, government agencies, statutory agencies, NGOs, civil society and mass media on promoting access to justice for women and children. The NLRD website is a knowledge hub for compilation of all laws, judgements and resource materials on violence against women and children in India. In the first phase, it will focus on the laws related to human trafficking, domestic violence, juvenile justice, rape laws, PCPNDT Act, honour crimes and victim compensation.

Endnotes

1. http://www.eldis.org/fulltext/Preventive Measures for Female Foeticide.pdf, last visited on 21st February, 2013.
2. 2003 8 SCC 398.
3. 2005 Cri.LJ 3408; 2005 (3) MhLJ 1131.
4. 2007 (9) LJSOFT (URC) 2; A.I.R. 2008 Bom. 29.
5. AIR 2005 Bom 26; 2005 (1) Bom. CR 595; (2005) 107.
6. 2009 CRi.L.J. 721.
7. 2008 1 GLR 239.
8. A.I.R. 2006 Utr 78.
9. A.I.R. 2008 P H 108.
10. Compilation and analysis of case laws on Pre-conception and Pre-natal Diagnostics Techniques (Prohibition of Sex Selection) Act, 1994.
11. Pradhan, Mandakini, Renu Singh, Manisha, Sarita Agrawal, "The Shortcoming of Prenatal Diagnostic Techniques Act", Department of Medical Genetics, Sanjay Gandhi Post Graduate Institute of Medical Science, Lucknow, India, 2004.

8

Role of Civil Society and Media in Preventing Female Foeticide

In an atmosphere like the present one, where the empowerment of women is endangered along with her dignity and integrity at stake, the only way out seems to be that of exclusive and strict legislations that bar further deterioration. This environment has thus given rise to certain segments of society who, suo moto take charge to help victims and make way for change. These organizations comprise of individuals to be collectively known as NGOs (non-governmental organizations).

8.1 Convention on the Elimination of All Forms of Discrimination against Women (CEDAW)

CEDAW, adopted in 1979 by the UN General Assembly, is often described as an international bill of rights for women. Consisting of a preamble and 30 articles, it defines what constitutes discrimination against women and sets up an agenda for national action to end such discrimination.

The Convention defines discrimination against women as "...any distinction, exclusion or restriction made on the basis of sex which has the effect or purpose of impairing or nullifying the recognition, enjoyment or exercise by women, irrespective of their marital status, on the basis of equality of men and women, of human rights and fundamental freedoms in the political, economic, social, cultural, civil or any other field".

By accepting the Convention, States commit themselves to undertake a series of measures to end discrimination against women in all forms, including the following:

- To incorporate the principle of equality of men and women in their legal system, abolish all discriminatory laws and adopt appropriate ones prohibiting discrimination against women;

- To establish tribunals and other public institutions to ensure the effective protection of women against discrimination; and
- To ensure elimination of all acts of discrimination against women by persons, organizations or enterprises.

The Convention provides the basis for realizing equality between women and men through ensuring women's equal access to, and equal opportunities in, political and public life—including the right to vote and to stand for election—as well as education, health and employment. State parties agree to take all appropriate measures, including legislation and temporary special measures, so that women can enjoy all their human rights and fundamental freedoms.

The Convention is the only human rights treaty which affirms the reproductive rights of women and targets culture and tradition as influential forces shaping gender roles and family relations. It affirms women's rights to acquire, change or retain their nationality and the nationality of their children. State parties also agree to take appropriate measures against all forms of traffic in women and exploitation of women. Countries that have ratified or acceded to the Convention are legally bound to put its provisions into practice. They are also committed to submit national reports, at least every four years, on measures they have taken to comply with their treaty obligations.

8.2 Civil Society including NGOs

NGOs in association with governmental organizations have made efforts to eliminate the problem of female foeticide. For example, in 2005, Swami Agnivesh, a child rights advocate, led a 2,000 km. interfaith pilgrimage through five of the worst afflicted states. They were welcomed by the leaders of over 40 towns with rallies and programmes to raise awareness about female foeticide. Similar awareness initiatives have taken place around the country. In Mumbai, an organization called "Population First" launched a five year campaign in 2005 with the slogan, "celebrate her life because she is precious". The programme engages Mumbai communities to alter social prejudices against girls. The

Campaign works with various stakeholders including NGOs, media, medical professionals, opinion makers, role models, youth icons and the communities. Smaller scale campaigns targeting the medical community have produced tangible results. Many religious leaders have been eager to join the fight against female foeticide. For example, Sikh leaders have committed to ex-communicate from the gurudwara, any individual who resorts to sex selection, and religious leaders in Delhi have aligned on the issue. [1]

In Gujarat, in 2005-06, the then Chief Minister Narendra Modi, started the *Beti Bachao* campaign. Year after year, the government has tried to appeal to diverse sections of Gujarat to understand and value the importance of a girl child in ways, unique to such sections.

The other role that a State can play is to strictly enforce laws and rules aimed at preventing this menace. The Pre-Natal Diagnostic Techniques Act, 1994 has been in place primarily to prohibit the practice of sex selection and sex determination with an aim to check female foeticide. Back in 2006, the Gujarat government, through a senior advocate and his instructing law firm, conducted seminars for various district health officers (DHOs) to prepare the paperwork and collate evidence under the complex PNDT Act in order to assist public prosecutors in securing convictions for violations. Shoddy work was found to be the primary reason for a glaring inability to secure convictions of rather obvious cases of malpractice.

Additionally, in order to plug several loopholes in the existing PNDT Act, the Gujarat High Court formulated directions based upon suggestions from the senior counsel for the government and other parties. The purpose was to keep the concerned DHO in the information loop on pregnancy related diagnostic issues. A gist of the directions being implemented today are listed below:

1. Every pregnant woman must be registered with the concerned DHO within two months of pregnancy with a unique code;

2. The Department of Health must issue pregnant women, a *Mamta* card without which the diagnostic sonography would not be conducted;
3. If a pregnant woman is advised to terminate pregnancy after having conducted an authorized diagnostic sonography, prior permission of the concerned DHO has to be obtained;
4. Within 10 days after a diagnostic sonography is conducted, medical practitioners must fill prescribed forms with detailed information on diagnostic sonography and any treatment/operations without disclosing details protected by patient privacy; and
5. The necessary paperwork as prescribed under the PNDT rules must be submitted by medical practitioners online, in addition to paper filing.

The Department of Health of the Government of Gujarat was asked to widely publicize these measures so that citizens of each district could be well-informed. However, there still exist a few ways by which errant medical practitioners have been able to circumvent the system, particularly with technological developments not known at the time this case was initiated in the Gujarat High Court in 2006.

For example, it has been found that, in many cases, illegal practices were conducted over the weekend and related data was erased from the machines. Since this data can be instantaneously wiped off without a tangible trace, such information is never included in the filings required under the PNDT Act.

To effectively counter such practices, the government counsel has suggested that Rule 3A in the PNDT Rules can be amended in a manner that any sonography machine imported into India or manufactured in India has an inerasable hard drive which stores data for the minimum period of two years as prescribed under the PNDT Rules. For existing machines, Gujarat has taken the help of the "Silent Observer" tool developed by IIT graduates that can be attached to sonography machines to monitor the activities.

Both the aforementioned roles played by the state and an overall increase in social awareness have resulted in decent improvements in the female-male ratio over the past five to six years in Gujarat. Undoubtedly, the problem, which has permeated itself with collusion at several levels since decades, requires participation from all sections of society such as community and religious leaders, NGOs, alert citizenry and medical professionals, in addition to the state. But, the beginning has been encouraging and, while, indeed, there is a long way to go, Gujarat continues to strengthen the framework required to effectively monitor the menace of female foeticide. [2]

Prenatal Diagnostic Techniques (Regulation and Prevention of Misuse) Act was enacted in 1994 by the Centre followed by similar Acts by several state governments and union territories of India during 1988 (after Maharashtra legislation to regulate prenatal sex determination tests), as a result of pressure created by Forum Against Sex-determination and Sex Pre-selection. But there was a gross violation of this Central legislation. In response to the public interest petition filed by Dr. Sabu George, Centre for Inquiry into Health and Allied Themes Mumbai, and MASUM fought on their behalf by the Lawyers Collective (Delhi); [3] the Supreme Court of India gave a directive on May 4, 2001 to all state governments to make an effective and prompt implementation of the Pre-natal Diagnostics Techniques (Regulation and Prevention of Misuse) Act (enacted in 1994 and brought into operation from January 1, 1996). Now, it stands renamed as "The Pre-conception and Pre-natal Diagnostic Techniques (Prohibition of Sex Selection) Act".

Pre-natal Diagnostic Techniques (Prohibition of Sex Selection) Act, 2003 tightens the screws on sex selection at pre-conception stage and puts in place a string of checks and balances to ensure that the Act is effective. [4] The Pre-natal Diagnostics Techniques (Regulation and Prevention of Misuse) Amendment Act, 2002 received the assent of the President of India on January 17, 2003. The Act provides "for the prohibition of sex selection, before or after conception, and for regulation of pre-natal diagnostic techniques for the purposes of detecting genetic abnormalities or metabolic disorders or sex-linked disorders and for the prevention of their misuse for sex determination leading to female foeticide and for matters connected therewith or incidental thereto".

Under the Act, a person who seeks help for sex selection can face, at first conviction, imprisonment for a 3-year period and be required to pay a fine of ₹ 50,000. The state medical council can suspend the registration of the doctor involved in such malpractice and, at the stage of conviction, can remove his/her name from the register of the council. The Pre-Natal Diagnostic Techniques (Regulation and Prevention of Misuse) Amendment Rules, 2003 have activated the implementation machinery to curb nefarious practices contributing to *missing girls.* According to the rules, all bodies under the PNDT Act, namely, genetic counselling centre, genetic laboratories or genetic clinic cannot function unless registered. [5] The Bombay Municipal Corporation has initiated a drive against the unauthorised determination of gender of the foetus as per the directive of the Ministry of Law and Justice. All sonography centres are required to register themselves with the appropriate authority—the medical officer of the particular ward. The registration certificate and the message that under no circumstances, sex of foetus will be disclosed are mandatory to be displayed. [6]

To deal with a problem that has roots in social behaviour and prejudice, mere legislation is not enough. Various activities have been undertaken to create awareness against the practice of pre-natal determination of sex and female foeticide. To implement the provisions of the Act, the help of media units like AIR, Doordarshan, Song and Drama Division, Directorate of Field Publicity, Press Information Bureau, Films Division and DAVP is also being sought. Workshops and seminars have been organized through voluntary organizations at state, regional, district and block levels to create awareness against this social evil. Cooperation has also been sought from religious leaders, as well as the medical fraternity to curb the practice.

A concerted effort involving all sections of the society is necessary to change the prevalent social thinking and remove the gender-based discrimination if the goal of a balanced sex ratio is to be achieved. Keeping this in view, the Government launched the "Save the Girl Child Campaign". One of its main objectives is to lessen the preference for a son by highlighting the achievements of young girls. To achieve the long-term vision, efforts are afloat to create an environment where sons and daughters are equally valued. Such efforts cannot take place in isolation or in relation to a single issue of female foeticide. They have to be integrated into the larger advocacy and communication efforts that are already taking place.

Framing a social problem in the formal and specific language of law has firstly, clearly defined all the key players and their roles in promoting the practice and, secondly, put in place, institutional mechanisms to enforce norms that will regulate the practice. Legislation and regulation provide a framework within which the role of multiple actors and institutions can be concretely measured and evaluated. For instance, regulation has a critical impact on the larger medical and pharmaceutical industry that has sprung up around reproduction in general and SD in particular, of which doctors are only a part.

The difficulties and gaps in regulating the use of technologies like obstetric ultrasound for SD should not become the basis for an argument against regulation. A number of measures can be taken to ensure effective implementation. For example, under both the MTP Act, 1971 and the PNDT Act, 1994, specific sites have been classified for legal provision of these services. Universal registration of these sites and listing of diagnostic equipment, granting licenses and requiring that they be prominently displayed, among others, could help curb misuse.

The PNDT Act can be the first step in a broader effort to regulate the private health care sector. The law, as currently implemented, fails in that it does not specify the role that has been played almost single-handedly by the private sector in spreading SD and SSA across the country. It is worth noting that SD was banned in all public facilities in the mid-seventies. Having discussed the usefulness of laws it is important to point out that they are at best a first step in addressing deep-rooted injustice. George (2002), one of the three petitioners of the PIL, pointed out that a law and effective use of the judiciary can bring pressure on the executive branch of the government to do a better job of monitoring use of these technologies, guide medical ethics that till date have been seriously lacking with regard to SD and SSA, and at the same time serve as a catalyst to address deep-rooted patriarchal norms within Indian society.

8.3 Role of Press and Media

Media plays a critical role in changing gender stereotypes. The approach to media strategy in India has been to use it as an instrument of change and to control its possible misuse. Media is encouraged to develop a code of conduct, professional guidelines, other self-regulatory mechanisms to remove gender stereotypes and promote a balanced portrayal of women and men.

The existing law on regulating content in the media is contained in different sources. Thus, Article 51A of the Constitution states that it shall be the duty of every citizen of India to renounce practices derogatory to the dignity of women. Similarly, Section 294 of the I.P.C. provides for penalties for obscene acts or conduct. The Indecent Representation of Women (Prohibition) Act, 1986 prohibits indecent representation of women through advertisement or in publications, writings, paintings, figures or in any other manner. The Act was enacted in the year 1986 and since then the issue of what is *obscene* has been a subject of great debate. The Act itself mostly revolves around how the object will affect society and the public morality rather than how it offends women.

The Indian Information Technology Act, 2000 has declared online pornography a punishable offence.

The role of the media in portraying women and the female gender as a whole leaves much to be desired. Press and the print media are generally found to unduly sensationalize traumatic events such as rape etc. thereby invading the privacy of the victim. Very few positive stories of girls/women are published who have stood up for their rights or are achievers. Similarly, the electronic media and films portray serial/films highly derogatory to women, glorifying subservience of the woman to her husband/in-laws, celebrating the birth of the boy child and portraying the disappointments of the family at the birth of the girl child. Eve teasing/sexual harassment is often a *fun* item in Indian films. As a result, the general populace is fed on a regular diet of stories/news that are highly gender abusive, thus reinforcing traditional views that the women are an inferior race and can be freely exploited.

The media has perforce to become gender sensitive and more responsible when portraying women and thus play a significant role in bringing about attitudinal changes in the society. A gender-friendly media policy needs to be formulated for this purpose.

Negative, violent and/or degrading images of women including pornography, stereotyped portrayals, have increased in different forms using new communication technologies in some instances, and bias against women remains in the media. Poverty, the lack of access and opportunities, illiteracy, lack of computer literacy and language barriers, prevent women from using the information and communication technologies, including the internet. Development of and access to internet infrastructure is limited especially in developing countries and particularly for women.

The lack of gender sensitivity in the media is evidenced by the failure to eliminate the gender-based stereotyping and the reinforcement of women's traditional role that can be found in public and private media. The continued projection of negative and degrading images of women in media communications is evident. The world-wide trend towards consumerism has created a climate in which advertisements and commercial messages often portray women primarily as consumers and target girls and women of all ages inappropriately. Advertisements of beauty products, magazines and beauty pageants mushrooming all over, have led to the creation of an image of an *ideal woman*.

Media policy needs to be gender proactive. There is a need to encourage media to project positive images and balanced portrayal of women and girls to enable attitudinal changes. The media policy should also help in generating awareness on gender issues and concerns so that the process of societal reorientation towards creating a gender just society gets widely disseminated.

8.3.1 Initiatives by Ministry of Information and Broadcasting

1. Implementation of specific enactments and laws to ensure better projection of women on television and films.
2. Promulgation of the code for commercial advertising on All India Radio and Doordarshan.
3. The Cable TV Network (Regulation) Act.
4. Promulgation of a code of conduct by the Indian Newspaper Society.
5. Review of all programmes before their telecast by Doordarshan to ensure that they are in accordance with the broadcast code that prohibits violence and vulgarity.
6. 50 percent representation of women is ensured in the Film Censor Board.
7. The Indian Information Technology Act has declared online pornography, a punishable offence.

8.3.2 Media as Catalyst of Social Change

1. The national network of Doordarshan provides 4.3 percent of the programming time to social education
2. A special programme cell has been given a daily slot to strengthen public service broadcasting around gender issues.

3. The University Grants Commission and the Indira Gandhi National Open University have initiated a knowledge based channel–Gyan Darshan—in which a series of programmes on issues like the role of the status of women, health and nutrition, education, social justice, environment and sustainable development have been commissioned and aired.
4. The All India Radio broadcasts special programmes for women, with focus on health, family welfare, nutrition, education etc.
5. The Directorate of Advertising and Visual Publicity organises publicity awareness on subjects like health and family welfare, women and child development, uplifting the girl child, education to creating public opinion against dowry, female infanticide, child labour and awareness about social welfare schemes and programmes.
6. The Directorate of Field Publicity also spreads messages on removal of social evils like dowry, chid marriage and rights of women.

Media has participated in the campaign and highlighted the problem through investigative reports and articles providing clinching evidence to prosecute the guilty. Media involvement, however, has not been limited to investigative reporting and exposure journalism.

In association with the Government and NGOs, the media has launched widespread awareness campaigns in the form of video spots on national and private television stations. One national network even presents a weekly TV series, which confronts the plight of the girl child.

Television show "Satyamev Jayate" touched upon one of the most critical issues plaguing India. Female foeticide is a menace, which has eroded not just sex ratio statistics, but the entire social fabric of the nation.

That a woman, the creator of life in this world, is given little importance with the distorted mentality prevailing across classes, castes, sects and faiths that the impending birth of a girl child is undesirable. The "Missing Women of Asia" is a well-documented reality which, as our Prime Minister has remarked, is a "national shame".

In this context, one of the episodes was instrumental in stirring the societal conscience using the sheer star power of Aamir Khan. While this is a society-created problem, and a complete eradication of it will only come about with a change in the prevailing mindsets, what role can governments play in curbing this menace?

The state has a two-fold role. Firstly, each MLA and MP, including Chief Ministers and Prime Minister can create awareness of the far-reaching disastrous consequences of this problem in his or her constituency and inspire them against its practice.

Secondly, all policies, schemes and programmes that are started by the government for upliftment of girl child should be properly implemented.

The state has a very important role to play in ensuring that positive steps are taken to eradicate this social problem and making sure that the women enjoy equal status as the men do in the Indian society.

The media should try making people aware about the declining sex ratio and make efforts to make people sensitive towards the problem of girl child.

Endnotes

1. Bijayalaxmi Pandey and Lalit Mohan Nayak, "Female Foeticide in India: Some Observations", Vol. 1, May 2012.
2. http://www.indiatribune.com/index.php?option=com_content&view=article&id=8870:the-menace-of-female-foeticide-gujarats-initiatives&catid=107:coverpage&Itemid=471, last visited on 16th March, 2013.
3. Asmita Basu, "Sex Selective Abortions", *Lawyers Collective*, Vol. 18, No. 11, November 2003, pp. 20-23.
4. Seema Kamdar, "Sex Selection Law Tightened", *Times of India*, 6th June, 2003.
5. "Handbook on PNDT Act, 1994", Department of Family Welfare, Government of India, for use by appropriate authorities in States/Union Territories, New Delhi, 2002.

6. Vibhuti Patel, "Sons Are Rising, Daughters Are Setting", *Humanscape*, September 2003.

9

Strategy to Checkmate Female Foeticide

9.1 Framework of Intervention

The findings of the present study point at male child preference as a pivotal factor in female foeticide. The study also reveals that the normative preference for the male child emanates from gender typed roles, male inheritance and descendency. Intervening factors such as penetration of the market, religious extremism, imposition of codes of conduct for women, identity assertions leading to control over female sexuality and reproduction and even piecemeal intervention for positive discrimination have led to the enhanced worth of the male child and while simultaneously increasing liability of the girl child. The framework of strategies needs to take into consideration both structural factors that promote male child preference and also extra venous factors that have enhanced the worth of the male child.

The gravity of the problem demands immediate measures to combat female foeticide. But the complexity and deep rootedness of the issue necessities a long-term intervention framework. The strategy thus needs to be broad-based from being only problem centered i.e. targeting the practice of female infanticide and infanticide to cripple the very processes (i.e. norms and values and other gender practices) that have been historically institutionalized and effect the adoption of preventive measures. In other words, a three-layered approach —behavioural modification, change in social moves and practices, and transformation of institutional and structural setting—has to be adopted. Not only should individuals and social relations be targeted but also the social structures need to be addressed.

This will mean that information and awareness generation

itself may only change or initiate a behaviour change in a particular section of the society. The state has to regulate activity so far considered private. Capacity building and incentives will encourage weakening of the existing gender social placements. However, for the vast majority, as is evident from the surveys, male child preference has not been combated by the existing policies, awareness of legal provisions or proclamations by the religious clergy denouncing female foeticide. The behaviour choices of the population are determined by social norms and values institutionalised in the family setting, in interpersonal relations, in religion and culture and promoted through the social, economic and political milieu. For instance, an earlier study had found that 37 percent of those who denounced sex determination tests were using other methods such as religious bigotry and prescriptions from quacks or *hakims* to beget a male child.

Although, the right to birth of a girl child may be ensured in a certain section of the population, yet the right to quality and dignified life continues to be negated due to the discrepant worth of the male and female child. Thus, if a girl child is allowed to be born because the community is God-fearing and does not want to be seen taking a life and will not also resort to female infanticide, yet indifference to the girl child can lead to cultural neglect and thereby the denial of life chances. The sex ratio will continue its march towards being more and more masculine.

9.2 Male versus Female Child

9.2.1 Male Child Preference:

- Male child is an old age insurance.
- Male child brings social status.
- Penetration of the market has appropriated male child preference to promote consumption patterns through large scale celebrations of birth, *lohri*, *mundan*, *namkaran* etc.
- Celebrating rituals associated with the birth of a male child and his life stages are becoming status symbols.

- Technology is differentially utilised to practise male child preference.

9.2.2 Girl Child as Liability:

- Perceived as the *other*, over which parents have no claims.
- Dowry exchange is crucial in preventing the birth of a girl child.
- Revivalism of the fundamentalist movement and identity assertions.
- Women perceived as the group's honour.
- Imposing codes of conduct.
- Small family norm has displaced the girl child.
- Segmented initiatives to promote women's development have marginalized the girl child.
- Property laws in peasant patrilocal society have resulted in increased dowry and resentment towards the girl child.
- *Shagun* scheme at the level of norm has endorsed the view that the girl child is a liability, therefore provided compensation for by government.

9.3 Intervention Strategy

Any strategy to combat female foeticide needs to address all factors that determine male child preference and those that enhance the worth of the male child. The core elements of patriarchy (gender typed roles, male descendancy and inheritance, defining the male as the earner and protector, the vanguard of family lineage and inheritor of resources and property) ensure the male child to be the preferred sex at birth. The initiation into each life stage revolves around these prototypes and reinforces them. This differentiation between male and female continues around the life cycle initiated by different institutions and practices at different junctures. Thus the coming of age of both male and female adolescents charter their respective responsibilities and functions in accordance with their gender placement.

Female mobility gets restricted, dress and conduct codes are imposed, as is earnest harnessing of capacities to be dictated towards being a home caretaker, procreator and nurturer. The male, on the other hand, is encouraged to acquire productive income earning skills. The institution of marriage and death-related practices form part of the gender determined constructs with unfolding of each life stage and the hegemony of the male is dictated. Therefore, intervention cannot be restricted to birth, pre-birth or post-birth activities that discriminate between a male and a female.

It is the entire life cycle and associated institutions (gender structures that attach a high value to the male child and low worth to a girl child), practice through differentiating roles have to be undermined. In other words, the male child preference does manifest starkly in the preferred birth of a male child, but the hegemonic importance of the male is instated at every juncture of life with different social mechanisms and processes supporting the difference. It has also been found that while patriarchy does ensure the importance of the male child with the male being the preferred child at birth, intervening external factors interlink with patriarchy to ensure that the girl child is received as a burden and the importance of the male child is enhanced. The penetration of the market has ensured that celebration for the birth of a male child; dowry exchange and associated marriage ceremonies have acquired the dimensions of status symbols.

Market forces have thus transformed normative rituals, practices or customs into an entity, valued for their material and resource worth. For instance, celebrations at the time of the birth of a male child are seen as a status symbol enhancing social worth of the family in terms of popularity, goodwill, in providing an occasion to display its opulence. The politics of fundamentalist extremism and identity assertion have glorified the female as the family's honour posing bodily restrictions in terms of appearance, codes of conduct and mobility. The added burden of visible control over female sexuality and reproduction has reinforced the sense of liability of a female while also targeting her for avenging honour.

These fundamentalist assertions continue to fuel the culture of violence in Punjab which promotes violence as a method of conflict resolution. This regenerates violent masculinities, be it for martyrdom or for heroism. Shedding blood for one's land or women has a mandate, increasing the value of protection—male to provide the protection over female. The culture of violence may perhaps even be providing acceptability to acts of violence including female foeticide.

Simultaneously, the adoption of the small family norm has displaced the girl child in this milieu of increasing importance of the male child. Other development initiatives such as property laws in the peasant patriarchal society and subsequent increase in dowry have also impacted the negative worth of the girl child. Implementation of schemes to provide positive discrimination to the female and the girl child, such as favourable labour laws have ousted women from the formal sector. The *Shagan* scheme which at the level of norm has endorsed the view that the girl child is a liability and therefore, the provision of compensation. These initiatives could be effective measures to check the discrepant male-female worth only when these are contextualised in a gender sensitive environment. In other words, simultaneous efforts at the level of practice, norms and values have to address the practice of differentiation between the male and the female.

9.3.1 Contextualising the Strategies: The strategy to combat female foeticide has to be contextualised as well as operationalised in consideration of gender inter-linkages. It is important to view the strategy and implement it in a holistic manner, rather than as an ad hoc initiative. While a particular agency may not be able to put into action the diverse aspects of the strategy, the consideration to the framework is a prerequisite. Thus, initiating common celebrations for the male and the female child must be done in a gender sensitized milieu, so that the need for capacity building of the female and undermining of role stereotyping is also addressed. The strategy involves incorporating changes in society that would promote an outlook that leads to empowerment of the community as a whole, and encourage a gender based response by pooling community resources. Combating female foeticide and infanticide hinges on empowering populations.

Empowerment involves combating prejudices and biases, building democratic norms, and at the same time providing community support, building relational communication and enabling economic independence. Empowerment further needs to evoke a gender based response that undermines social constructs and gender subjectivities and allows interaction between specific populations and their social surroundings. These include grassroots organisations, religious leaders, opinion-making sections, teachers, community leaders and NGOs.

9.3.2 Mainstreaming a Gender Perspective: A gender-based response takes into consideration the different access and participation that men and women have in society. Its aim of providing full opportunities to both the sexes focuses on weakening the fixed roles, differential responsibilities, social expectations and the status of men and women. It is directed at combating gender values, norms and practices that subordinate women and manifest in incidents of violence against women. In many societies, gender shapes the female ideal by encouraging submissiveness and passivity that curtail decision-making by women and confine them to the household and promote sexual submission. Masculine ideals such as male dominance that encourage husbands to be forceful and boys to adopt an aggressive, at times even predatory, sexual behaviour, and encourage substance abuse and alcohol also need to be understood and tackled.

9.3.3 Creating and Accessing Entitlements: Empowering specific groups needs to focus on developing their human capacity and skills by providing infrastructural resources to enable them to use the skills. They need to be sensitised and provided with skills that enable them to take informed decisions, acquire better communication skills and capacity to generate income along with the requisite infrastructure and services for their human development. Thus, access to health, education, productive skills and communication skills are the prerequisites. This should also involve health functionaries who, because of the cultural bias in favour of the male child may encourage indiscriminate use of ultrasound for sex determination. For the higher health professionals, pressure to invoke professional ethics to curtail the misuse of technology may be a better strategy.

9.3.4 Building Community Support: People do not live in isolation. They are surrounded by the family, health workers, teachers, community and religious leaders, NGOs etc. All these people may have different perceptions, needs, attitudes and preferences, with varying levels of awareness and sensitivity to gender issues. Moreover, these sections continuously interact with one another to produce the dominant norms, values and ideals of society. In this particular context, the needs, aspirations, and problems of a specific population are to be dealt with. Primarily, their attitudes and values have to be taken into consideration. For instance, in the case of women in the slums, it may not be possible to effectively intervene if they do not have information on income generating avenues, guidance or support from government departments, or if the community does not support them in activities or programmes they are participating in. Also, it needs to be recognised that different sections of the community may have comparative advantage over the others in one or more spheres such as information, resources, skills or knowledge. Experienced NGOs or health services can perhaps provide the best technical information and services. Religious leaders may have the highest moral authority.

Community leaders can provide support and credibility to programmes and women may need the support of their families. Forging partnerships between these sections of the community for growth and change in the traditional attitudes and norms becomes essential. It is through the support of these partnerships that the needs and aspirations can be fulfilled and the community gender sensitised.

An integrated approach targets immediate needs through

short-term strategies in the context of long-term needs in targeting social change. Studies have shown that communities are responsive to change when it is backed by information, skills and opportunities.

9.3.5 Enshrining the Female's Right to Life: The unfavourable conditions for women, reflected in the adverse sex ratio, have been persisting over the decades, changing their form in accordance with the change in economic and social conditions. Given the historically adverse sex ratio in various backward states, increasing atrocities and continuing male-female disparities, the modern technology of pre-natal sex selection cannot be held responsible for the imbalance in male-female numbers. No doubt, technology in the form of sex determination tests has given added boost to male child preference, but male child preference is rooted in culture. This preference and its manifestation included female infanticide at the turn of the century, prior to the invention of pre-natal diagnostic techniques. Female foeticide is another form of denying the right to birth and life in addition to traditional mores and female infanticide. This change of form and the visible adoption of scientific technology may give the misleading impression that pre-natal sex selection techniques are in fact the cause of adverse sex ratio.

9.4 Identification of Issue

The issue raised by the decline of sex ratio is not that the female's right to birth is violated. Rather, it is the non-existence of the female's right to life. The historically adverse sex ratio and the socio-cultural legitimacy of traditional methods (visits to *hakims*, *deras*, pilgrimages for boon of a male child) that register the selection of the male child over the female, is proof enough of the lack of right to birth for the girl child. The need is, therefore, to enshrine the right of birth to the girl child and then the right to life. After the right to birth, if the right to life is denied in the shape of female infanticide, cultural neglect or the blatant use of violence as in dowry death, it will again lead to an imbalance in the sex ratio. This calls for a holistic strategy that deals with unfavourable status of the female in its entirety.

9.4.1 Systematically Targeting Female Foeticide: To answer life enhancing mechanisms resulting in life depriving outcomes lies in the understanding that pre-natal diagnostic techniques do not exist in a vacuum but function in accordance with the social conditions of patriarchy. [1] In other words, female foeticide occurs because there is a male child preference in the society. The male child preference emanates from the perceived higher relative worth of the male than that of the female. Not only does the male have a normative hegemony, culturally accumulated through the practice of discrimination against the girl child in favour of the male, the male has more developed capacities than the female. He is more skilled, promotes the lineage and is an old age insurance for parents. In order to combat this male child preference, the female productive worth in society has to be enhanced.

9.4.2 Evoking Legal Measures with the Support of the Community: There is a need for arresting the rapid decline in the child sex ratio and legal measures have been adopted by the state in this regard. However, these legal remedies can only be implemented through mobilisation of the community and its subsequent support. For this, some sections of the society would respond to awareness generation of laws and initiate behaviour change by appealing to rationality while to other sections gender sensitization and the increased worth of the girl child would diminish male child preference. However, for the large majority, awareness generation or sensitisation would not succeed in weakening the male child preference which is dictated by social norms and values institutionalised in the family setting, in interpersonal relations and in religion and culture. For this section of the society, the norms, values and practices that have been historically institutionalised need to be attacked.

9.4.3 Promoting the Composite Status of the Female: Individual adherence and institutionalisation of the gender ideology both provide invisibility to gender violence. The widespread invisibility of gender violence and its various forms can be inferred from the prevalence of gender typed roles, values and norms that justify male child preference, allocation to the female, the role of nurturer and caretaker and acceptance of gender practice such as payment of dowry. This widely accepted gender ideology produces partial and fragmented understanding of the assumptions, processes and even actions of the gender system. Moreover, this inadequate understanding isolates the events from the assumptions and processes of the gender system and reduces them to mere problematic aberrations. Thus, female foeticide is assumed to be the problem and not the male child preference; dowry demand and harassment are targeted for correction, while promoting dowry exchange; subjugation of the wife is accepted while intervention is sought for wife bashing. Thus, the situation blurs some of the most pervasive forms of gender violence and solutions that revolve around welfare or relief and are unable to empower women.

9.5 Policy Framework to Combat Female Foeticide

9.5.1 Providing Visibility to Gender Violence: There is need for sensitizing the community to issues relating to gender justice and women's development. The policy needs to ensure sensitization to all forms of deprivation, discrimination and atrocities. Socialisation of the norms and values of patriarchy makes certain forms of injustice invisible. Thus, expression of male child preference through traditional methods remains invisible and is not perceived as denial of the right to life or as violence against the female gender.

9.5.2 Promoting Role Identity in Lieu of Gender Role Stereotyping: Human biology in the existing socio-biological context has only affixed the biological function of procreation to the two sexes. All other roles are socially determined. Thus, functions such as rearing the children, earning for the family, performing household chores, taking part in familial, social or political decision-making can be undertaken by members of the either sex. Individual capacities can be harnessed according to the situation and need. Thus, role fluidity will help in combating the restricted and inferior social placement on the basis of sex. If women are to be productive earners, they will be encouraged to imbibe market valued skills that bring high remuneration.

9.5.3 Promoting Women as Productive Beings: Given the increasing economic demands, earning an income has become necessary for all individuals. However, women even upon entering the wage market have been constrained by the primary role assumptions of child rearing and housekeeping. They earn only to supplement the earnings of the menfolk since the burden of household chores and child-care continues to be their sole responsibility.

Earning only as a supplementary function results in the marketing of existing skills which are domestic in nature. If the women's potential as workers is harnessed according to their capacities i.e. if they learn skills before entering the work force as part of their education like the males, and are encouraged to learn market valued skills, then more women will join the labour force in various skilled categories with corresponding remuneration. This then will promote productive participation of women in all social spheres, creating an increased social worth of the females.

9.6 Legal Strategies

- Review and reframe the existing laws on pre-natal diagnostic techniques to clearly include in its ambit, sex selection techniques also. Only sex detection techniques are included in the Pre-natal Diagnostic Techniques Act, 1994.
- Target the clinic and organisations that spread awareness regarding sex selection techniques for having male child, including community patrolling squads.
- Enforce the ban on sex determination techniques through

community policing.

- Spread legal literacy regarding women's rights.
- Build pressure for legal reforms in areas of gender violence (domestic violence including rape in marriage and honour revenge to be legally addressed).
- Initiate state regulation to discourage opulent celebrations such as the birth of male child, *lohri*, *namkaran*, *mundan* ceremonies and marriages (for instance, if more than 100 guests have been entertained in such celebrations, then it should be mandatory to file an income tax return).

9.6.1 Awareness Campaign:

- Provide information regarding the extent of female foeticide and infanticide which are thought to be brutal acts and no longer practiced.
- Raise concerns regarding the impact of the falling sex ratio in the area, especially its repercussions on gender.
- Generate awareness that practice of male child preference is a form of gender abuse. To visit *deras*, *pirs*, temples, gurudwaras for begetting a male child is not different from visiting sex detection clinics.
- Awareness regarding government schemes, NGO initiatives etc. to promote the status of the girl child.
- Spread awareness that recurring abortions are harmful to maternal health.
- Launching a campaign with the help of religious organisations to advocate women's control over their bodies in terms of reproduction and sexuality.
- Encourage the community to celebrate customs, rituals and practices of all life stages without differentiating between males and females.
- Spreading the awareness that a small family need not only include male children irrespective of sex selection.
- Encourage the clergy to denounce *mannats* and blessings only for male children at *deras* and gurudwaras.
- Awareness regarding various schemes that the government has initiated for women's uplift. These should include

schemes that are: (a) welfare-oriented, (b) developmental and (c) income-generating.

- Awareness regarding human sexuality.

9.6.2 Sensitisation:

- Sensitise grassroot organisations, especially panchayats and *mahila mandals* to gender issues. This should include:
- Questioning the legitimacy of male child preference.
- Targeting the dowry system rather than only dowry harassment and dowry deaths.
- Promoting the value of women as productive workers.
- Promoting role fluidity.
- Delinking the value of honour from control over women's sexuality.
- Promoting the principles of social policing and social fencing within the community to act as an instrument to curtail female foeticide and infanticide.
- Form community patrols to check clinics and health workers from performing female foeticide.
- Challenging exhibition of dowry, celebrations for the birth of a male child as a status symbol.
- Undermine the legitimacy of male child preference.

9.6.3 Initiatives for Capacity Building:

- Equipping women with productive skills.
- Initiating micro credit and micro enterprise for income generation.
- Providing women with access to health services and community resources.
- Initiate informed decision-making in families and in the community to promote democratic relationships.
- Boost democratic processes within GROs, especially panchayats.
- Establishing a network with grassroots organisations, line departments and the community.
- Developing skills of communication and decision-making in the community and among the women in particular.

- Providing infrastructure and community mobilisation on gender and empowerment issues.

Today, what is of concern is not just the decreasing sex ratio but the piecemeal intervention being implanted for gender development. To focus on female foeticide as the cause of the adverse sex ratio, amounts to trivialising the issue. The need is to counter male child preference, introduce role fluidity, and provide sensitization to the gender system and visibility of atrocities. The state needs to set up an inter-departmental task committee to develop an action plan and evaluate ongoing programmes on the basis of the framework of intervention.

9.7 Initiatives by Central and State Governments

9.7.1 Kishori Shakti Yojna (KSY): KSY seeks to empower adolescent girls, so as to enable them to take charge of their lives. It is viewed as a holistic initiative for the development of adolescent girls. The programme through its interventions aims at bringing about a difference in the lives of the adolescent girls. It seeks to provide them with an opportunity to realize their full potential.

This scheme is a redesign of the already existing Adolescent Girls (AG) Scheme being implemented as a component under the centrally sponsored Integrated Child Development Services (ICDS) Scheme. The new scheme dramatically extends the coverage of the earlier scheme with significant content enrichment, strengthens the training component, particularly in skill development, aspects aimed at empowerment and enhanced self-perception. It also fosters convergence with other sectoral programmes, addressing the interrelated needs of adolescent girls and women.

The broad objectives of the Scheme are to improve the nutritional, health and development status of adolescent girls, promote awareness of health, hygiene, nutrition and family care, link them to opportunities for learning life skills, going back to school, help them gain a better understanding of their social environment and take initiatives to become productive members of the society.

9.7.2 Cradle Baby Scheme: The 'Cradle Baby Scheme' was introduced in the year 1992 in the Salem district of Tamil Nadu. This scheme has been recognized all over India and other countries. Under this Scheme, cradles are placed at locations like hospitals, primary health centres, orphanages and children homes which are likely to receive female children which are abandoned by their parents due to social circumstances like debts, future financial commitments, females being prone to sexual exploitation etc.

Children received at the cradle points are handed over to reception centres for rehabilitation. The babies received through this scheme in the reception centres are rehabilitated and handed over to the licensed adoption agencies to be taken care and also to enable them to find a family who are willing to adopt these children.

The 'cradle baby scheme', brainchild of Chief Minister Jayalalithaa, will be extended to Cuddalore, Ariyalur, Perambalur, Villupuram and Tiruvannamalai districts as the 2011 Census has revealed a fall in the child sex ratio in these districts.

Cradle baby centres will be set up at a cost of ₹ 47.45 lakh and each centre will have a superintendent, an assistant nurse, an assistant and other workers. The centres will have adequate stock of milk powder, medicine and clothes. Besides, cradles will be placed at hospitals, primary health centres and children homes to receive girl children.

She said the cradle baby scheme, launched in Salem district in 1992 with a view to eradicating female infanticide, was later extended to Madurai, Theni, Dindigul, Dharmapuri, Erode and Namakkal districts in 2001 when she became chief minister of the State for the second time. As many as 188 centres in these districts were equipped with incubators, life-saving drugs, refrigerators, gas connections, bed sheets and clothes for children. The government also organised camps, seminars and conferences to create awareness of female infanticide.

The scheme was appreciated not just in India, but across the world. Many girls were saved from the clutches of death and were later given in adoption; they grew up in families and received good education and are leading a prosperous life.

9.7.3 Ladli Scheme: This scheme by the Government of India envisages a payment in the name of a girl child annually, which is kept as a fixed deposit which can then be collected with interest when the girl reaches 18 years of age.

Without mention, there are always certain conditions applied. In this case, the parents should be Delhi-based or should have been living there for a minimum of 3 years. The child should also be born in Delhi. It is a scheme for girls whose parents earn less than ₹ 1,00,000 per annum. The conditions sound easy don't they? Thousands of people can fulfil it. But let us see, how the Ladli Scheme has helped the National Capital.

It can be seen that the scheme did not help in boosting up the female sex ratio in Delhi and there are various reasons for that. Firstly, getting cash in hand is what the poor wanted which is not the case with Ladli Scheme; this is why the families are not much revved up about it. Also, the corruption that prevails in India makes it extremely difficult for the poor to get registered.

But the most significant hurdle in the way of the scheme was the lack of information. Many people do not know of the existence of such a scheme even now even though it was launched in 2008 in Delhi. And the people who do know are quite misinformed which is why there are not many people registering under it.

Also, instead of helping the people who actually need such support, politicians are known to pocket the money spent by the government for such purposes. Thus, what started of as a brilliant scheme towards egalitarian growth of the society in terms of gender issues, ended up being a complete fiasco.

The only thing that can be done to change the present situation is to make people aware of the scheme and encourage people to demand their rightful share. The time taken to complete the official work involved should be reduced so that it is easy for the people to register. This can be done when corruption is kept in check. All this, if implemented properly, would help the Ladli Scheme to achieve its objectives of correcting the lop-sided sex ratio.

9.7.4 Beti Bachao: It is a campaign in India to end the gender selective abortion of female foetuses, which skewed the population towards a significant under representation of girls in some Indian states. The "Beti Bachao" campaign is supported by human rights group, non-governmental organisations, and the state and local governments in India.

Beti Bachao activities include large rallies, poster campaigns, wall paintings, bill boards, and television commercials and short animations and video films. Celebrities such as video director—Jagmeet Bal and bollywood actress Priyanka Chopra, have become involved in "Save the Girl Child" initiatives.

The Beti Bachao campaign is supported by numerous medical organisations in India, including the Indian Medical Association.

Government support at the state level has provided funding for Beti Bachao publicity activities in particular. The expenditures related to the campaign have been a source of political controversy in Madhya Pradesh, which launched its official 'Beti Bachao Abhiyan' campaign in 2012.

The campaign has reported some success in parts of India. In 2009, it was reported that in Gujarat, rate of female births increased from 802 to 882 for every 1,000 male births. Beti Bachao activities were credited with this improvement.

Apart from the programmes mentioned above, the Government of Himachal Pradesh launched a scheme named "Beti Hai Anmol" and for below poverty line families to incentivize the birth of girl child up to two children and encourage families to place scholarship up to 12th standard through conditional cash transfer. As per the state's latest evaluation on sex ratio, the state has improved from 904 females for 1,000 males in 2008 to 922. Uttarakhand state has also given a fixed deposit amount of ₹ 5,000 to a newborn girl child from BPL families under the "Nandadevi Kanya Scheme" to stop female foeticide in the state.

Endnote

1. The development of science is not neutral but is directed to serve and frequently to validate the dominant interest which an ideology is legitimating and supporting. V.L. Allen, 1974, *Social Analysis,* London: Longman, p. 229.

10

Women and Health

Discrimination against women and girls impinges upon their right to health and manifests itself in the form of worsening health and nutrition indices. Thus, India continues to grapple with unacceptably high maternal mortality rate (MMR), infant mortality rate (IMR) and increasing rates of anaemia, malnutrition, HIV/AIDS among women.

Women also disproportionately lack access to health services. Inaccessibility of health centres and poverty prevent them from getting timely medical aid. Absence of toilets and drinking water adversely impacts their health.

Inadequacies of clean cooking fuels adversely impacts women and children's work burden, health and nutrition.

Women and girls spend a great deal of time gathering fuel, adversely affecting their productivity and education. Use of firewood and inferior fuels such as weeds or crop wastes leads to smoke-related ailments including respiratory diseases, cancer and cataracts resulting in blindness.

10.1 Health Needs of Women

Women and girls in India face a crisis of growing health needs. From the moment of conception to the end of life, the challenges to the female sex are enormous, especially those who are poor; suffer from multiple exclusions, including caste, class, geographic isolation and tribal status. Health policies have few specific strategies for improving access to marginalized groups.

Malnutrition begins during infancy and sets in motion a life long cycle of poor health. Over half of all Indian women suffer from anaemia, which acerbates maternal morbidity. More women die of maternal death related causes in India than in any other country in the world. Women as a whole are especially susceptible to many diseases because of their poor nutritional standards and discriminatory practices in health inputs right from their birth.

Furthermore, every form of violence against women has steadily increased including rapes, dowry murder and domestic violence. Despite the alarming health crisis of women and girls, the national policy focus prioritizes family planning and reproductive health without addressing underlying issues such as women's low participation in decision-making, which adversely affects their health status. It is noteworthy that the leading killer of women in India is tuberculosis. Yet due to the focus on maternal and reproductive health this fact is little known and there are no gender-specific policies or programmes in place with regard to this disease.

10.2 HIV/AIDS

HIV in India is spreading from high-risk groups to the general population in many areas, and from urban to rural areas. Women are increasingly becoming the face of the HIV epidemic and there are biological, social, legal, cultural, political and economic factors that make them more vulnerable to HIV/AIDS. These factors, in turn, have an impact on women's access to services, resources, and information. Women have limited ability to negotiate safer sex and the risk and reality of sexual violence also means an increased risk of HIV transmission through unprotected non-consensual sex. In India, testing for the HIV virus is rare until symptoms set in. The numbers suffering from HIV/AIDS are therefore likely to be far higher than estimated. Once HIV/AIDS enters the home, family budgets are reversed forever because of loss of income earning opportunities and expenditure on medical care. Women are the major caregivers in most cases.

A multi-sectoral, decentralized, gender-sensitive and community-based health policy is needed. Effective strategies that address the relationships between gender and HIV/AIDS require a focus on gender within health care in general. There is perhaps an urgent need that the response to the HIV/AIDS epidemic be made multi-sectoral and be integrated into comprehensive, decentralized, participatory community-based health services. A focus on increasing women's ability to access preventive and treatment and care services is crucial.

10.3 Reproductive Health

The human rights of women include their right to have control over and decide freely and responsibly on matters related to their sexuality, including sexual and reproductive health, free of coercion, discrimination and violence. Equal relationships between women and men in matters of sexual relations and reproduction—including full respect for the integrity of the person—require mutual respect, consent and shared responsibility for sexual behaviour and its consequences.

Reproductive health is a state of complete physical, mental and social well-being—and not merely the absence of disease or infirmity—in all matters relating to the reproductive system and to its functions and processes. Reproductive health therefore implies that people are able to have a satisfying and safe sex life and that they have the capability to reproduce and the freedom to decide if, when and how often to do so. Implicit in this last condition is the right of men and women to be informed and to have access to safe, effective, affordable and acceptable methods of family planning of their choice, as well as other methods of their choice. In line with the above definition of reproductive health, reproductive health care is defined as the constellation of methods, techniques and services that contribute to reproductive health and well-being by preventing and solving reproductive health problems. It also includes sexual health, the purpose of which is the enhancement of life and personal relations, and not merely counselling and care related to reproduction and sexually transmitted diseases.

Bearing in mind the above definition, reproductive rights embrace certain human rights that are already recognized in national laws, international human rights documents and other consensus documents. These rights rest on the recognition of the basic right of all couples and individuals to decide freely and responsibly the number, spacing and timing of their children and to have the information and means to do so, and the right to attain the highest standard of sexual and reproductive health. It also includes their right to make decisions concerning reproduction free of discrimination, coercion and violence, as expressed in human rights documents. In the exercise of this right, they should take into account the needs of their living and future children and their responsibilities towards the community. The promotion of the responsible exercise of these rights for all people should be the fundamental basis for government- and community-supported policies and programmes in the area of reproductive health, including family planning.

Reproductive health eludes many of the world's women because of: (a) inadequate levels of knowledge about human sexuality and poor-quality reproductive health information and services, (b) prevalence of high-risk sexual behaviour (c) discriminatory social practices, (d) negative attitudes towards women and girls and (e) limited power many women and girls have over their sexual and reproductive lives. Adolescents are particularly vulnerable because of their lack of information and access to relevant services in most countries. Older women and men have distinct reproductive and sexual health issues which are often inadequately addressed.

10.4 Changing Pattern of Lifestyle Illness

India has made rapid strides in the health sector since Independence. With increased coverage and better access to health facilities, life expectancy in India has risen over the past 60 years. As per the Census 2011, the life expectancy for women was 72.6. As the life span increases, the incidence of chronic diseases is set to overtake infectious diseases. As many studies have pointed out, there are signs that India is entering the epidemiological transition with a change in disease patterns from infectious to chronic, degenerative and non-communicable diseases. This is attributed to improved nutrition, immunisation, and improved access to primary health care. In urban areas, more women are succumbing to newer lifestyle-related illnesses like diabetes, hypertension, cardiovascular and cancer.

A related issue is the fact that women in urban areas are often confined to the house and participate in the economy as home-based workers. To improve their conditions, more visibility is needed on the nature of the work and production system and the implications these might have for appropriate interventions.

10.5 Women and Ageing

Demographic ageing is a global phenomenon. With a comparatively young population, India is still poised to become home to the second largest number of older persons in the world. The asymmetry in the population pyramid with males outnumbering females as a whole and females outnumbering males at the upper end of the age spectrum is a peculiar feature of the Indian population.

There is lack of disaggregated data to assess the number of services availed of by aged women and their impact. The Government has committed itself to providing social security for the aged woman. The discrimination and subordination that the old women suffer, the glaring difference in education and literacy, income differentials between men and women are being looked into by Government for state intervention.

10.6 Specific Micronutrient Deficiencies in India

Some of the specific micronutrient deficiencies in the country which are of a magnitude that causes public health concerns are described below.

10.6.1 Iron Deficiency Anaemia (IDA): IDA is the most widespread micronutrient deficiency in the world affecting more than a billion people. It affects all age groups irrespective of gender, race, caste, creed and religion with higher incidence among vulnerable groups in developing world. Anaemia is associated with increased susceptibility to infections, reduction in work capacity and poor concentration. In India, this silent emergency is rampant among women belonging to reproductive age group, children and low socio-economic strata of the population. IDA reduces the capacity to learn and work, resulting in lower productivity and loss of wages, limiting economic and social development.

Anaemia in pregnant women leads to adverse pregnancy outcomes such as high maternal and neonatal mortality, low birth weight, increased risk of obstetrical complications, increased morbidity and serious impairment of the physical and mental development of the child. Anaemia remains one of the major indirect causes of maternal mortality in India. In children, anaemia causes low scholastic skills leading many of them to be below average in classes or premature dropping out from schools. It also triggers increased morbidity from infectious diseases.

It is also seen that children born to mothers who were illiterate or who belonged to scheduled castes/tribes were more likely to be anaemic than their counterparts. Further, children born to moderately and severely anaemic mothers were also anaemic, reflecting the consequences of poor maternal health status on the health of the children. Research studies have suggested that severe iron deficiency anaemia during the first two years of life, when the brain is still developing, may cause permanent neurological damage adding further sense of urgency to the current efforts to prevent iron deficiency anaemia in children.

The current strategy, included as part of Reproductive and Child Health Programme (RCH) under National Rural Health Mission, recommends that pregnant and lactating women, infants, school children and adolescents should be targeted in the Nutritional Anaemia Prophylaxis Programme as per the recommended dosage.

10.6.2 Iodine Deficiency Disorders (IDDs): IDDs are a major public health problem for populations throughout the world, particularly for pregnant women and young children. They are a threat to the social and economic development of countries. The most devastating outcomes of iodine deficiency are increased pre-natal mortality and mental retardation. Iodine deficiency is the greatest cause of preventable brain damage in childhood which is the primary motivation behind the current worldwide drive to eliminate it. The main factor responsible for iodine deficiency is a low dietary supply of iodine. It occurs in populations living in areas where the soil has low iodine content as a result of past glaciations or the repeated leaching effects of snow, water and heavy rainfall. Crops grown in this soil, therefore, do not provide adequate amounts of iodine when consumed.

Goitre is the most visible manifestation of IDDs. In severely endemic areas, cretinism may affect up to 5-15 percent of the population. While cretinism is the most extreme manifestation, of considerably greater significance are the more subtle degrees of mental impairment leading to poor school performance, reduced intellectual ability and impaired work capacity.

IDDs have been recognized as a public health problem in India since the 1920s. No State in India is completely free from IDDs. A third of all children in the world that are born with IDD-related mental damage live in India.

Indian National Goitre Control Programme (NGCP) was started in 1962 with a focus on the goitre belt in the country. However, the programme of universal iodization was introduced only in 1984, when all edible salt in the market was required to offer 30 ppm (parts per million) iodine at the production level. This was legalized through the PFA (Prevention of Food Adulteration) Act, 1988 that also banned the availability of crystalline salt (non-iodized) as an edible product. It was accepted variably by the different States, some putting only a partial ban and others none at all.

Based on the recommendations of the Central Council of Health, the Government took a policy decision to iodise the entire edible salt in the country by 1992. Since 1992, the National Iodine Deficiency Disorders Control Programme (NIDDCP) is the new name given to the erstwhile National Goitre Control Programme. This change has been effected with a view to cover the wide spectrum of iodine deficiency, such as mental and physical retardation, deaf-mutism and cretinism, under the programme. Due to various research reports, the Central Government lifted the ban on the sale of non-iodized salt in 2000. The States chose to retain or revoke the ban depending upon their own assessment. In 2005, a country-wide universal ban on sale of non-iodized salt for human consumption was again been promulgated by the Central Government.

10.6.3 Vitamin A Deficiency (VAD): Vitamin A is an important micronutrient for maintaining normal growth, regulating cellular proliferation and differentiation, controlling development, and maintaining visual and reproductive functions. Vitamin A Deficiency is one of the major deficiencies among lower income strata population in India. Human beings cannot produce this micronutrient in the body itself. Hence, it has to be externally provided. This deficiency is seen greater in pre-school children and pregnant and lactating women due to higher need for this micronutrient. In severe cases it can even lead to total blindness.

VAD has been recognized as a major controllable public health and nutritional problem. An estimated 5.7 percent children in India suffer from eye signs of vitamin A deficiency. Recent evidence suggests that even mild vitamin A deficiency probably increases morbidity and mortality in children, emphasizing the public health importance of this disorder.

Way back in 1970, a National Programme for Prevention of Nutritional Blindness was initiated to fight this deficiency. The beneficiaries of this programme were pre-school children (1-5 years). Further, the programme was modified in 1992 to cover children in the age group of 9 months to 3 years only. Presently, Vitamin A supplementation exists as an integral component of RCH programme which is a part of National Rural Health Mission. Ministry of Health and Family Welfare, Government of India, issued guidelines to the States in November 2006 extending the programme to cover children up to 5 years.

10.7 National Health Policy, 2002

The Department of Health has formulated the National Health Policy (NHP), 2002 which was approved by the Cabinet in 2002. The National Health Policy, 2002 aims at achieving an acceptable standard of good health amongst the general population of the country and has set the goals for the next two decades.

Areas of attention in the Tenth Five Year Plan (2002-07) included the reorganization and restructuring of existing health care infrastructure at primary, secondary and tertiary levels so that they have the capacity to render health care services to the population residing in well defined geographical areas and have appropriate referral linkages with each other. Appropriate delegation of powers to panchayati raj institutions to ensure loçal accountability of public health care providers, horizontal integration of all aspects of the current vertical disease control programme, including supp-lies monitoring, IEC, training and administrative arrangements, development of appropriate two-way referral system utilizing information technology, exploring alternative systems of health care financing, and defining the role of various stakeholders—government, private and voluntary sectors—are the other focus areas.

10.8 Sarva Swasthya Abhiyan (SSA)

The Tenth Five Year Plan (2002-07) indicated the dismal picture of the health services infrastructure and emphasized the need to invest more on building good primary-level care and referral services. The Plan emphasized on restructuring and developing the health infrastructure, especially at the primary level. The Plan highlighted the importance of the role of decentralization but did not state how this would be achieved. Programme-driven health care was in focus. Verticality and technical solutions were given more importance than the comprehensive primary health care. The multi-sectoral approach that is much needed for a vibrant health system had not been well thought out.

Eleventh Five Year Plan (2007-12) envisaged inclusive growth by introducing National Urban Health Mission (NUHM) which along with National Rural Health Mission (NRHM) will form Sarva Swasthya Abhiyan (SSA). NRHM was launched for meeting health needs of all age groups and reduce disease burden across rural India. NUHM was launched to meet the unmet needs of the urban population. NUHM based on health insurance and public-private partnership will provide integrated health service delivery to the urban poor. Initially, the focus will be on urban slums. NUHM will be aligned with NRHM and existing urban schemes. Besides, Sarva Swasthya Abhiyan aims for inclusive growth by finding solutions for strengthening health services and focusing on neglected areas and groups.

10.9 National Rural Health Mission (NRHM)

NRHM was launched on April 12, 2005, to provide accessible, affordable and accountable quality health services to the poorest households in the remotest rural regions. The thrust of the Mission was on establishing a fully functional, community owned, decentralized health delivery system with inter-sectoral convergence at all levels, to ensure simultaneous action on a wide range of determinants of health like water, sanitation, education, nutrition, social and gender equality. Under the NRHM, the focus was on a functional health system at all levels, from the village to the district.

The Mission aims to provide universal access to equitable, affordable and quality health care which is accountable and at the same time responsive to the needs of the people. The Mission is expected to achieve the goals set under the National Health Policy and the Millennium Development Goals.

To achieve these goals, NRHM facilitates increased access and utilization of quality health services by all, forge a partnership between the Central, State and the local governments, set up a platform for involving the PRIs and the community in the management of primary health programmes and infrastructure and provides an opportunity for promoting equity and social justice. The NRHM establishes a mechanism to provide flexibility to the States and the community to promote local initiatives and develop a framework for promoting inter-sectoral convergence for promotive and preventive health care. The Mission has also defined core and supplementary strategies.

10.9.1 Strategies of NRHM:

A. Core Strategies: These are the following:

1. Train and enhance capacity of panchayati raj institutions (PRIs) to supervise and manage public health services.
2. Promote access to improved health care at household level through the accredited social health activist (ASHA).
3. Health plan for each village through village health committee of the panchayat.
4. Strengthen sub-centre through an untied fund to enable local planning and action and more multi-purpose workers (MPWs).
5. Strengthen existing PHCs and CHCs and provision of 30-50 bedded CHC per lakh population for improved curative care to a normative standard (Indian Public Health Service Standards defining personnel, equipment and management standards).
6. Prepare and implement an inter-sectoral district health plan prepared by the district health mission, including drinking water, sanitation, hygiene and nutrition.
7. Integrate vertical health and family welfare programmes at national, state and district levels.

8. Technical support to national, state and district health missions for public health management.
9. Strengthen capacities for data collection, assessment and review for evidence-based planning, monitoring and supervision.
10. Formulate transparent policies for deployment and career development of human resources for health.
11. Develop capacities for preventive health care at all levels for promoting healthy life styles, reduction in consumption of tobacco and alcohol, etc.
12. Promote non-profit sector particularly in underserved areas.

B. Supplementary Strategies: These include the following:

1. Regulation of private sector including the informal rural practitioners to ensure availability of quality service to citizens at reasonable cost.
2. Promotion of public private partnerships (PPP) for achieving public health goals.
3. Reorienting medical education to support health issues including regulation of medical care and medical ethics.
4. Effective and viable risk-pooling and social health insurance to provide health security to the poor by ensuring accessible, affordable, accountable and good quality health care.

10.9.2 Five Planks of the National Rural Health Mission:

1. The Mission is expected to address the gaps in the provision of effective health care to rural population with special focus on 18 States, which have weak public health indicators and/or weak infrastructure.
2. The Mission is a shift away from the vertical health and family welfare programmes to a new architecture of all inclusive health development in which societies under different programmes will be merged and resources pooled at the district level.
3. The Mission aims at effective integration of health concerns with determinants of health like safe drinking water, sanitation and nutrition through integrated district plans for health. There is a provision for flexible funds so

that the States can utilise them in the areas they feel are important.

The Mission provides for appointment of accredited social health activist (ASHA) in each village and strengthening public health infrastructure, including outreach through mobile clinics. It emphasizes involvement of the non-profit sector, especially in the under served areas. It also aims at flexibility at the local level by providing for untied funds.

5. The Mission, in its supplementary strategies, aims at fostering public-private partnerships; improving equity and reducing out of pocket expenses; introducing effective risk-pooling mechanisms and social health insurance; and taking advantage of local health traditions.

In the Eleventh Five Year Plan, the emphasis under NRHM was not on numerical achievements only but also on Indian Public Health Service Standards and enforcement of guidelines for improving the functioning of infrastructure being strengthened and created. It was felt that the mission directors, both at the Centre and the States, should be officials with public health background, supported by the civil service cadres.

NRHM has successfully provided a platform for community health action at all levels. Besides merger of Departments of Health and Family Welfare in all States, NRHM has successfully moved towards a single state and district level health society for effective integration and convergence. Through a concerted effort at decentralized planning through preparation of district health action plans, NRHM has managed to bring about intra-health sector and inter-sectoral convergence for effectiveness and efficiency. In all the States, specific health needs of people have been articulated for local action.

With the establishment of public institutions like the village health and sanitation committees (VH&SCs), hospital development committees and PRI-led committees, it is the civil society to which the health system is being made increasingly accountable. Through untied and flexible financing, NRHM is trying to drive reforms that empower local communities to make their own decisions. It is thus a serious effort at putting people's health in people's hands.

10.10 Janani Suraksha Yojana (JSY)

To change the behaviour of the community towards institutional delivery, the Government of India, under NRHM in 2005, modified the National Maternity Benefit Scheme (NMBS), from that of a nutrition-improving initiative to the JSY. The scheme has the dual objectives of reducing maternal and infant mortality by promoting institutional deliveries. Though the JSY is implemented in all States and UTs, its focus is on States having low institutional delivery rate. The scheme is 100 percent centrally sponsored and integrates cash assistance with maternal care. It is funded through the flexi-pool mechanism.

While the JSY scheme is meant to promote institutional delivery, it has to take two critical factors into account, one being that India does not have the institutional capacity to receive the 26 million women giving birth each year, and the other being that around half of all maternal deaths occur outside of delivery, during pregnancy, abortions and postpartum complications. If institutions are preoccupied with handling the huge numbers of normal childbirths, there will be inevitable neglect of life-threatening complications faced by women. They will be compelled to vacate beds in the shortest time. Consequently, complications during pregnancy and after childbirth will not be given attention. Second, JSY money sometimes does not reach hospitals on time, and as a result, poor women and their families do not receive the promised money.

10.11 Family Planning and Welfare

As per the Census of India, 2011, the population of India as on March 1, 2011 stood at 1210 million, with males at 624 million and females at 586 million. Viewed globally, India constitutes 17 percent of the world population. India is following the demographic transition pattern of all developing countries from initial levels of *high birth rate-high death rate* to the intermediate transition stage of *high birth rate-low death rate* which manifests in high rates of population growth, before graduating to *low birth rate-low death rate* stage.

The current high population growth rate is due to: (a) the large size of the population in the reproductive age-group, (b) higher fertility due to unmet need for contraception and (c) high wanted fertility due to prevailing high IMR.

The goal of population stabilization can be achieved only when child survival, maternal health and contraception issues are addressed simultaneously and effectively. Actual success in containing the growth of population would, however, depend upon· (a) publicly-related support from community leaders, (b) resources available for the family welfare programmes, (c) efficiency and accountability in the States health system for ensuring effective delivery of services to citizens and (d) women's education and status in the family. All these inputs have so far not been uniformly available to the required extent for the family welfare programmes, thereby not allowing the optimal benefits to be reaped from the same.

10.11.1 Family Welfare in the National Population Policy (NPP), 2000: NPP adopted in February 2000 affirmed the commitment of the Government towards stabilizing the population of the country by providing for its citizens voluntary and informed decisions about their family size. The policy envisaged certain national socio-demographic goals to be achieved by 2010 for paving the way for a stable population in the country by 2045, at a level consistent with the requirements of sustainable economic growth and social development. It also provided a policy for advancing goals and prioritizing strategies during the next decade, to meet the reproductive and child health needs of the people of India, and to achieve net replacement levels of fertility (total fertility rate = 2:1) by 2010.

It was decided to relocate the National Population

Stabilization Fund (NPSF) from the National Commission on Population to the Department of Family Welfare. The NPSF was created with core funding of ₹ 100 crore from Government of India and will invite funds from the voluntary and corporate sectors.

An empowered action group (EAG) was constituted in the Ministry of Health and Family Welfare with Union Minister for Health and Family Welfare as Chairman on March 20, 2001. The EAG aimed at assisting States with weak socio-demographic indicators to attain the goals listed in the National Population Policy, 2000. In the first instance, the States of Bihar, Uttar Pradesh, Madhya Pradesh, Rajasthan, Odisha, Jharkhand, Uttaranchal and Chhattisgarh were chosen for focussed attention.

Population Census 2011 showed a decline in the sex ratio in the age group 0-6 years in several States. For the country as a whole the child sex ratio is 914 girls per 1,000 boys which is much less than 927 recorded in the 2001 Census. The Government is keen to strengthen the implementation mechanism of Pre-Natal Diagnostic Techniques (Regulation and Prevention of Misuse) Act, 1994.

The Reproductive and Child Health Programme (RCH) was launched on October 10, 1997 which combines fertility regulation, safe motherhood, child survival and reproductive tract infections (RTI)/sexually transmitted infections (STI). This programme is primarily implemented through the primary health care infrastructure.

Vitamin A deficiency, which can lead to blindness, has been prevalent in the country, especially among the pre-school children. Under the programme for prevention and control of vitamin A deficiency among children, five doses of vitamin A are administered to all children less than 3 years of age.

Iron deficiency (anaemia) is widely prevalent not only in women of child-bearing age but also in young children. The National Family Health Survey-II (1998-99) revealed that 74.3 percent children under the age of 3 years were anaemic. There is a marginal difference in the prevalence in the rural and urban areas. While 75.3 percent of rural children were found to be anaemic, the prevalence in urban children was 70.8 percent. Iron folic acid tablets containing 20 mg of elemental iron and 0.1 mg of folic acid are provided at the sub-centre level.

The agenda for population stabilization is multi-sectoral which necessitates decentralization and convergence across sectors. In cooperation with State Governments, the Department of Family Welfare is bringing about a convergence between the NGOs, the self-help groups, *zila saksharta samitis* and panchayati raj institutions, to improve integrated service delivery at community and household levels.

10.12 Nutrition Support

Although the country has been able to eliminate nutritional deficiency syndrome like pellagra, beriberi, scurvy etc. yet chronic energy deficiency among adults, under-nutrition among children and micronutrient deficiencies are still prevalent across all section of the population. The country has adopted a multi-sectoral and multi-pronged strategy to combat these problems and to improve the nutritional status of the population.

One half of the children under the age of 5 years in India are moderately or severely malnourished, 30 percent of newborn children are significantly under weight and nearly 60 percent of women are anaemic. Under the Integrated Child Development Scheme (ICDS), the Department of Women and Child Development implements the food supplementation programme for improving nutritional status of mothers and children. Ministry of Health and Family Welfare implements programmes for tackling major micronutrient deficiencies such as vitamin A and iodine deficiency etc.

To address the needs of under-nourished infants and children below 3 years, 15 percent of the total additional central assistance (ACA) is earmarked for the nutrition component under the Pradhan Mantri Gramodaya Yojana

(PMGY). ACA under the nutrition component of PMGY is an additionality for providing nutrition to children in 0-3 years. States are required to ensure that all below poverty line (BPL) children in 0-3 years are registered for PMGY and provided requisite nutrition.

The programme of Nutritional Support to Primary Education, popularly known as Mid-day Meal Scheme, was launched in 1995 as a fully-funded Centrally Sponsored Scheme. Under this scheme, all children in primary schools in government and government-aided schools are covered. Ideally, a hot meal is provided to the children at school for 10 months in a year. The foodgrains are delivered directly at the district level by the Food Corporation of India, under instructions from the Department of Education in the Government of India.

The Prime Minister, in his Independence Day speech on August 15, 2001 announced the setting up of National Nutrition Mission (NNM). Under this Mission, subsidized foodgrains are made available to adolescent girls and expectant and nursing mothers, belonging to below-poverty-line families. NNM is headed by the Prime Minister and its executive committee is under the Human Resource Development Minister.

To sum up, considerable achievements have been made over the last 65 years to improve health standards; such as in life expectancy, child mortality, infant mortality and maternal mortality. Small pox and guinea worm have been eradicated and there is hope that poliomyelitis will be contained in the near future. Nevertheless, problems abound. Malnutrition affects a large proportion of children. An unacceptably high proportion of the population continues to suffer and die from new diseases which are emerging apart from continuing and new threats posed by the existing ones. Pregnancy and childbirth related complications also contribute to the suffering and mortality.

India has to deal with rising costs of health care and

growing expectations of the people. The challenge of quality health services in remote rural regions has to be urgently met. Given the magnitude of the problem, there is the need to transform public health care into an accountable, accessible and affordable system of quality services.

Special attention needs to be given to the health of vulnerable groups like adolescent girls, women, children, older persons, disabled and primitive tribal groups. The contribution of the private sector in providing primary, secondary and tertiary services should be enhanced through various measures including partnership with the Government. Good governance, transparency and accountability in the delivery of health services should be ensured through involvement of panchayati raj institutions (PRIs), community and civil society groups.

11

Women and Education

Education is a key intervention in initiating and sustaining processes of empowerment. Good quality education can help women and marginalized communities to: (a) improve their status, (b) enable them to have greater access to information and resources and (c) challenge various forms of discrimination.

Education helps strengthen democratic processes as it allows for greater and more equitable participation. Being educated leads to greater self-confidence and self-esteem. It enables engagement with development processes and institutions of governance from a position of strength. Poor women from socially disadvantaged communities are invariably not literate and therefore find themselves at a disadvantage when participating in development processes.

There is an increased awareness that education is one of the most valuable means of achieving gender equality and the empowerment of women. Education is seen as a critical factor in breaking the inter-generational cycle of transmission of poverty. The power of education lies not just in imparting formal literacy, but rather in the acquisition of skills that enable access to multiple literacy—economic, legal, health, political and media etc.

It is, however, important to recognise that while being literate or educated is necessary for empowerment, it does not automatically ensure it. For that, a society needs an education system which is of good quality and promotes critical thinking. From the perspective of gender this means that education and literacy should enable women and girls to critically analyse their situations, raise questions about their subordination and help them make informed choices. It is well-known that the institution of schooling is an important site for socialisation that actually reinforces rather than challenges patriarchy and gender discrimination. It is in this context that the content and pedagogy of education become critical considerations.

The focus of educational planning is generally on formal education but this is only one dimension of the educational provisioning, especially when needs of deprived women are under consideration and empowerment of women is the main objective.

11.1 Education for All

The 86th Constitutional Amendment Act, 2002 made free and compulsory education a justiciable fundamental right for all children in the 6-14 year age group. The Government of India is committed to realising the goal of elementary education for all and bridging of gender and social gaps by 2010. The *Sarva Shiksha Abhiyan* (SSA), launched in 2001-02, is the national umbrella programme that is spearheading the universalisation of elementary education through a community-owned approach, with a specific focus on the provision of quality education. SSA has relied on the Education Guarantee Scheme (EGS) and Alternative and Innovative Education (AIE) which are specially designed to provide access to school-less habitations. The scheme provides flexible strategies for out-of-school children through bridge courses, residential camps, drop-in-centres, summer camps, remedial coaching etc. to bring these children to school.

Though the content of education and classroom pedagogy are critical to altering gender and other social relations it has not been paid the attention it deserves. Efforts to make curricula gender-sensitive have been undertaken but can be considered initial attempts as they have remained largely at the level of removing stereotypes or increasing visibility and have not looked at gender in terms of social relations.

Problems related to the representation of marginalized communities continue to exist and contribute to the deep sense of alienation of these communities from the mainstream education system and a reason for children dropping out. Sexuality is addressed in a problematic manner in educational materials. It is either related to population or reproductive health or seen as a problem associated with promiscuity and shame. Classrooms need to be transformed into spaces that can help girls think critically. Discriminatory practices based on identity-based prejudices need to be monitored and stopped. Corporal punishment, which is widespread, needs to be checked. The role of the teacher is naturally crucial in this context.

11.2 Sexual Harassment, Violence and Women's Education

Sexual harassment and violence against girls and young women within educational institutions is widespread but under-reported. There are systematic mechanisms to gather data that indicate the extent of the problem. While some universities have formulated guidelines and established mechanisms to deal with sexual harassment, many educational institutions still do not have policies. Though technically the guidelines should cover schools, no efforts have been made to implement the guidelines in schools where sexual harassment is fairly common but is rarely reported. One only has the media (print and electronic) to rely on for such information. Another area that has not received much attention is the impact of conflict and communal and sectarian violence on education. Communal and sectarian violence and long-term conflicts severely impact opportunities for girls and women's education. In volatile situations girls are kept away from schools.

In parts of India, like the North East and Kashmir, that have been experiencing conflict for several years, the ground level situation reveals that prolonged violence has negatively impacted the education systems there and the education opportunities for women and girls in various ways. Dropout rate of girls is high because of fear, insecurity, restricted mobility, displacement, migration etc. School participation and quality of education for girls is impacted by measures to control women's sexuality and mobility, like diktats imposing a dress code by religious bodies, militants or separatist groups.

In such situations, schooling and other educational

interventions can bring about a semblance of normalcy and prevent alienation from the mainstream. No systematic efforts have been made to understand and monitor the impact of conflict on education, especially women and girls. There are no policy guidelines on how to respond to the impact of violence and conflict. There are no mandated special provisions to deal with the particular problems arising out of such situations. Education provisioning, from gender perspective, should find a place in any policy on internal displacements and associated relief and rehabilitation measures.

11.3 Elementary Education

Within the education sector, elementary education has been given the highest priority in terms of sub-sectoral allocations and a number of schemes launched by the Central Government to meet the needs of the educationally disadvantaged. A brief description of select programmes for elementary education is as follows.

11.3.1 Sarva Shiksha Abhiyan (SSA): Launched in November 2000, SSA is a comprehensive programme and the main vehicle for providing elementary education to all children. The goals of SSA are the following:

1. All children in School, Education Guarantee Centre, Alternate School, Back-to-School camp by 2005.
2. Bridge all gender and social category gaps at the primary stage by 2007 and at elementary education level by 2010.
3. Universal retention by 2010.
4. Focus on elementary education of satisfactory quality with emphasis on education for life.

SSA, implemented in partnership with the States, addresses the needs of 192 million children in the age group of 6-14 years. It covers 9.72 lakh existing primary and upper primary schools and 36.95 lakh teachers.

SSA is the culmination of all previous endeavours and experiences in implementing various education programmes. SSA has been the single largest holistic programme addressing all aspects of elementary education covering over one million elementary schools SSA has brought primary education to the doorstep of millions of children and enrolled them, including first generation learners, through successive fast track initiatives in hitherto unserved and underserved habitations.

11.3.2 Kasturba Gandhi Balika Vidyalaya Scheme (KGBVS): KGBVS was launched in July 2004 to set up 750 residential schools at elementary level for girls belonging predominantly to the scheduled castes, scheduled tribes, other backward classes and minorities in educationally backward blocks (EBBs).

All 750 KGBVs have now been sanctioned by the Government of India, with 117 KGBVs (15.6 percent) allocated to blocks with substantial minority population. A minimum of 75 percent of the enrolment in KGBVs is reserved for girls from the target groups and the remaining 25 percent is open for girls belonging to the below poverty line (BPL) category.

11.3.3 District Primary Education Programme (DPEP): Started in 1994, DPEP, an externally aided project, aimed at the holistic development of primary education covering Classes I to V. It had specific objectives of reducing the dropout rate to less than 10 percent, reducing disparities among gender and social groups in the enrolment to less than 5 percent and improving the level of learning achievement compared to the baseline surveys. However, these ambitious targets could not be achieved. Still, DPEP brought about a sea change in the implementation of school education programme with its decentralized approach and focus on community participation. At its peak, DPEP covered 273 districts in 17 States.

11.3.4 National Programme of Nutritional Support to Primary Education: Launched on August 15, 1995 with the objective to boost the Universalisation of Primary Education by impacting upon enrolment, attendance, retention and nutritional needs of children studying in class I-V. During

2012-13, 10.68 crore children (elementary level) were covered in 12.12 lakh schools. 10.45 crore children were covered in 11.58 lakh schools during 2013-14.

11.3.5 Pradhan Mantri Gramodaya Yojana: This programme was launched during 2000-01 and envisages Additional Central Assistance for basic minimum services in certain priority areas. The scheme has six components covering elementary education, primary health, rural shelter, rural drinking water, nutrition and rural electrification.

A minimum of 10 percent of ACA for all components except nutrition (for which it is 15 percent) has been fixed. The allocation for the remaining 35 percent of ACA would be decided by the States and UTs among the components of the Scheme, as per their priorities. Funds for elementary education sector under PMGY are utilized to further the goal of Universalisation of Elementary Education.

11.3.6 National Programme for Education of Girls at Elementary Level (NPEGEL): It is an important component of SSA. NPEGEL provides additional support by way of girl-child friendly schools, stationery, uniforms, etc. for girls' education in educationally backward blocks (EBB), and in other areas for elementary education of under privileged and disadvantaged sections.

EBBs are blocks with female literacy below, and gender gap above, the national average. Apart from EBBs, NPEGEL is also implemented in blocks of districts which are not covered under EBBs but have at least 5 percent SC/ST population and where SC/ST female literacy is below 10 percent, and also in select urban slums. In the Tenth Five Year Plan, an amount of ₹ 1,064.80 crore was earmarked for this programme.

Launched in July, 2003 as a focused intervention aimed at enhancing girls' education, NPEGEL provides for development of a "model school" in every cluster with more intense community mobilisation and supervision of girls' enrolment in schools. Gender-sensitisation of teachers, development of gender-sensitive learning materials and provision of need-based incentives like stationery, workbooks and uniforms are some of the objectives under NPEGEL. It is being implemented in about 3,164 educationally backward blocks in 25 States.

Under NPEGEL, around 31,450 model schools have been developed and 1.97 lakh teachers gender-sensitised. Over 51,345 early childhood care and education (ECCE) centres are being supported in areas not covered by Integrated Child Development Services (ICDS) scheme to help free girls from sibling care responsibilities and attend schools. Free uniforms have been given as a direct educational incentive to about 2 crore girls in educationally backward blocks.

11.3.7 Education Guarantee Scheme and Alternative and Innovative Education (EGS&AIE): Another important component of SSA is the EGS&AIE. It is specially designed to provide access to elementary education to children in school-less habitations and out-of-school children. It supports flexible strategies for out-of-school children through bridge courses, residential camps, drop-in centres, summer camps, remedial coaching, etc.

11.3.8 Mahila Samakhya (MS): MS, an externally aided project for women's empowerment, was started with Dutch assistance in 1989. Since 2005-06 it is being funded by GOI. The programme endeavours to create an environment for women to learn at their own pace, set their own priorities and seek knowledge and information to make informed choices. It has strengthened women's abilities to effectively participate in village level education programmes. The programme is implemented in 9 states covering 83 districts. The States of M.P. and Chhattisgarh have registered MS societies through which the programme is initiated. It provides for vocational and skill development as well as educational development of adolescent girls and women in rural areas.

11.3.9 Prarambhik Shiksha Kosh (PSK): Department of Elementary Education and Literacy issued orders on November 14, 2005 constituting Prarambhik Shiksha Kosh

(PSK) to receive the proceeds of the education cess imposed through Finance (No. 2) Act, 2004. PSK is a separate, dedicated, non-lapsable fund to be maintained by the Ministry of Human Resource Development.

11.3.10 Problem Areas: In education, the elementary sector is besieged by numerous systemic problems such as inadequate school infrastructure, presence of single-teacher schools, high teacher absenteeism (especially in rural areas), large-scale teacher vacancies, inadequate equipment, etc. This brings into focus the role of decentralization and people's participation in the provision of basic services.

It is essential that control over schools and teachers should be transferred to local bodies, having a direct interest in teacher performance. This has also been highlighted as an area of emphasis in the Tenth Plan.

The National Policy on Education (NPE), 1986, as modified in 1992, emphasised three aspects in relation to elementary education:

1. Universal access and enrolment.
2. Universal retention of children up to 14 years of age.
3. A substantial improvement in the quality of education to enable all children to achieve essential levels of learning.

NPE emphasised that education must play a positive and interventionist role in correcting social and regional imbalance, empowering women, and in securing a rightful place for the disadvantaged and the minorities. Government is firmly committed to providing education for all, the priority areas being free and compulsory elementary education, covering children with special needs, eradication of illiteracy, education for women's equality, and special focus on the education of SCs/STs and minorities.

11.4 Adult Education

Literacy is the most essential prerequisite for individual empowerment. A new thrust was given to adult literacy in the National Policy on Education (NPE), 1986 and the Plan of Action

1992, which advocated a three-pronged strategy of adult education, elementary education and non-formal education to eradicate illiteracy. The National Literacy Mission (NLM) was launched on May 5, 1988 as a Technology Mission to impart functional literacy to non-literates in the country in the age group of 15-35 years in a time-bound manner. This age-group is the focus of attention because it is in the productive and reproductive period of life. NLM was set up with an initial target to make 80 million persons literate by 1995, which was later enhanced to 100 million by 1997 and the revised target was to achieve a threshold level of 75 percent literacy by 2007.

The Total Literacy Campaign (TLC) has been the principal strategy of NLM for eradication of illiteracy in the target group. These campaigns are area-specific, time-bound, volunteer-based, cost effective and outcome-oriented. They are implemented by *zila saksharata samities* and district level literacy societies.

Keeping pace with its endeavours, campaigns and programmes, the NLM has strengthened and revitalized the States Literacy Missions which have been imparted greater autonomy. They now have the authority to plan, implement and monitor literacy programmes and sanction continuing education programmes at the State level. The NLM has also come to recognize the great potential that NGOs have in furthering its programmes and schemes. Given the major role, NGOs are now allowed to receive funds from *zila sakshara samities* and actually run continuing education centres. The *jan shikshan sansthans* have expanded their outreach and are also catering to the rural segment by offering vocational training courses.

At present, 595 districts are covered under the TLC and continuing education programmes is being implemented in 328 districts. In addition, 221 *jan shikshan sansthans* have been set up to provide vocational training to the neo-literates and backward sections of the society. There are 25 state resource centres established for providing academic and technical resource support for the literacy programmes.

NLM has accorded priority for the promotion of female literacy. According to 2001 Census, 47 districts in the country have female literacy rate below 30 percent. Most of these districts are concentrated in Bihar, Jharkhand, Uttar Pradesh and Odisha. Special innovative projects have been taken up to raise the level of female literacy in these areas. Special efforts have been made to target female Panchayati Raj functionaries and make them literate.

11.4.1 Jan Shikshan Sansthan (JSS): The objective of JSS Scheme is educational, vocational and occupational development of socio-economically backward and educationally disadvantaged groups of urban/rural population, particularly neo-literates, semi-literates, SCs, STs, women and girls, slum dwellers, migrant workers etc. By linking literacy with vocational training, JSSs seek to improve the quality of life of the beneficiaries. JSSs offer around 284 different types of vocational courses—from candle and agarbatti making, to computer training and hospital/health care. The total number of JSS is 221.

11.4.2 Weaknesses of Adult Education Programmes: The constraints in the implementation of adult education programmes include inadequate participation of the State Governments, low motivation and training of voluntary teachers/preraks, lack of convergence of programmes, and weak management and supervision structure for implementation of NLM. Besides, the funding for various components of NLM schemes is inadequate and the level of community participation is also low.

12

Conclusions and Suggestions

Mahatma Gandhi, the father of the Nation said, "man and woman will attain equality only when the birth of a girl is celebrated with as much joy as in the case of a boy". [1]

All children have the right to be protected against all forms of discrimination, harm, loss and deprivation. Protection measures must address social, psychological, physical, mental, emotional and material risk, danger and damage. Protection must also safeguard and defend children against discrimination of all kinds, including neglect. Girl children are especially at risk of violation of their protection rights simply because they are girls. In societies and communities where women are not respected, the girl child is not valued. In many parts of India, she is in danger of being unwelcomed even before birth and is denied fair care and treatment right from birth and through the childhood years. Much of what should be considered maltreatment is socially regarded as the 'normal/accepted' way to treat a girl child in the home or community. The girl child stands unprotected from the traumatic potential of much that is considered customary. From the stand point of human rights, this places her in need of both preventive and corrective protection.

Keeping in view the dimensions and magnitude of this problem, we can see that it is a social problem that can be increased or decreased by society only. The society includes our families, social institutions, educational institutions, social organizations, NGOs, doctors, government, administration, media, police, political and religious leaders. They are the guards and protectors of the society. Hence, their contribution and efforts regarding female foeticide and infanticide is very important to effectively tackle the problem of female foeticide and bring this menace to an end. The following suggestions are made in this regard:

- Sensitization should be done in all departments of universities and training should be conducted to enable the campaign to reach the remotest of villages. Cultural practices such as celebrations and festivals should be utilized for campaigns and that communication must reach the masses.
- There is a need to form linkages—socio-cultural-health-economic-political and legal—in order to fight the declining sex ratio.
- In private institutions, over which no effective control could be exercised, they should not be issued licenses for carrying out pre-natal diagnostic procedures and techniques. Only government hospitals should be facilitated with these services.
- Monitoring of Act's implementation is required.
- Offensive advertisements must be reported and action must be taken.
- Notice boards at clinics/hospitals/nursing homes must state that sex determination is punishable.
- Ultrasound machines and other sex determination techniques should be sold only to registered clinics coupled with affidavits/undertaking not to use them for sex determination.
- Men and women of our society need counselling to change their mindset.
- All men should know that they are responsible for determining the sex of the child and not only women.
- Mentality of people should be changed. Killing of the foetus is against human rights.
- Sex selective abortions have a bad effect on the health of the women—should be conveyed to the people through media.
- Licenses of the doctors who perform sex selective abortions should be cancelled.
- Value your daughter. Each one of us can change our immediate environment by treating our daughters equal to our sons. If each of us looks at the girl child with a changed

mindset, it will break the prevailing social apathy.

- Changing mindset includes the attitudes and thinking process for both girls and boys. Girls need, and should expect, equal access to education, nutrition, health, employment and productive resources. Boys and men should perceive girls not as subservient beings but as empowered individuals who are equal partners.
- On the basis of literature review and empirical evidences, the Government of India should start a central flagship programme for BPL families through conditional cash transfer in the form of fixed deposit (*Kisan Vikas Patra*) in favour of new born girl child up to 2nd girl child to combat female foeticide in the country. The guidelines to encash the fixed money should be on written document i.e. only the eligible candidate (the girl child) can encash the deposit after completion of 18 years.
- Medical audits should be made mandatory and conducted on regular basis and the DMO, DC and SP need to be proactive on the issue.
- The offender under the amended PNDT Act could be arrested without warrant and this needs to be widely publicized. State should punish the guilty and in this way the law can be an instrument of change.
- Sensitization of the youth towards this issue was seen as non-negotiable. The existing forums that have youth participation, like the National Service Scheme, Nehru Yuva Kendras and other youth centric agencies must have female foeticide on their agenda. The central/state governments need to facilitate such agendas. Resident welfare Associations could be given a social policing role to: (a) keep track of the growth of such clinics, (b) discourage the use of sex determination and selection and (c) aid in social audits.
- Anganwadi workers, SHGs and other women groups at the community level could be given training to monitor such issues and counselling facilities should be made available to pregnant women at all maternity clinics and hospitals by

well-trained professional counsellors.

- Review of existing research along with an understanding of redressal mechanisms and knowledge of public opinion is necessary. The research must incorporate an action programme. The research needs to be used as a means for identification of areas of intervention and not solely for academic purposes.
- The religious dimension to the problem needs special attention. Encouragement to more qualitative research studies are required to understand cultural norms that lead to sex selection and female foeticide by which new strategies can be made for further policy formulation.
- Media should show positive images of women rather than negative images to enhance their status. Print and electronic media if used in a controlled manner, can lead to desired results in solving the problem of female foeticide.

To conclude, it is suggested that only framing of laws would not solve the menace of female foeticide until it is properly implemented by the appropriate authorities. There should be a concerted action between the legislature, which makes the laws after analysing the problem and judiciary which is given the task of interpreting the law made. Punishments should be made stricter, and the guilty should not escape. All people in the society should join hands and fight towards injustice caused to women and aim at an overall development of women in all spheres. Media should work for attainment of rights of women, making the people sensitive towards this issue and ensuring that the state performs the duties imposed upon it. We all, as members of the society, save girl child as they are the future of tomorrow and development of girl child would directly lead to progress of the country.

Endnote

1. *Social Welfare*, Vol. 55, No. 7, October 2008, p. 2.

Bibliography

Bibliography

Primary Sources

Constitution of Eire, 1983.

Indian Penal Code, 1890.

Medical Termination of Pregnancy Act, 1971.

Pre-Natal Diagnostic Techniques (Regulation and Prevention of Misuse Act), 1994.

West German Constitution, 1949.

Secondary Sources

Books

Bonda, A. "The Impact of Constitutional Law on the Protection of Urban Human Life: Some Comparative Remarks", Lucknow, 1977.

Gaur, K.D., "Criminal Law and Materials", 3rd edition, Universal Law Publishing Co., Delhi, 1999.

Miller, B., "The Endangered Sex: Neglect of Female Children in Rural North India", Ithaca, New York and London, Cornell University Press, Ithaca, NY, 1981.

Patel, Tulsi, "Sex Selective Abortions in India", Sage Publications, New Delhi, 2006.

Patel, Vibhuti, "Indian Women's Struggle to Survive: Campaign against Foeticide", New Delhi, 1994.

Ranganathan, Sarala and Saddiqi Ehtesham Fatima, "Handbook on Women and Human Rights: A Guide for Social Activists", Kanishka Publishers and Distributors, Delhi, Part 1, 2001.

Rao, Mamta, "Law Relating to Women and Children", Eastern Book Company, 2nd edition, Lucknow, 2008.

Raymond, J.G., "In Women as Wombs", Spinifex, Melbourne, 1994.

Sachdeva, D.D.R., "Social Welfare Administration in India", Kitab Mahal, Allahabad, 1998.

Saxena, Sarojini, "Femijuris", India Publishing Company, New Delhi, 1994.

Saxena, Shobha, "Crimes against Women and Protection Laws", Deep & Deep Publishers, New Delhi, 1995.

Articles

Bandyopadhyay S. and Singh, A., "History of Son Preference and

Sex Selection in India", *Western Bulletin,* Indian Institute of History of Medicine, Hyderabad, 2006.

Basu, Asmita, "Sex Selective Abortions", *Lawyers Collective,* Vol. 18, No. 11, November 2003.

Bose, S. and Trent, K., "Socio-Demographic Determinants of Abortion in India: A North-South Comparison", *Journal of Biosocial Science*, 2006.

George, S.M., "Sex selection/Determination in India: Contemporary Developments", *Reproduction and Health Matters*, 2002.

George, Sabu and Dahiya, Ranbir S., "Female Foeticide in Rural Haryana", *Economic and Political Weekly,* Vol. XXXIII, No. 32, August 8-14, 1998.

Kamdar, Seema, "Sex Selection Law Tightened", *Times of India,* June 6, 2003.

Kolloor, P., "Female Infanticide: A Psychological Analysis", *Grass Roots Action*, April 1990.

Nakra, Neeru and Dhingra, Rajni Malhotra, "Female Foeticide", *National Capital Law Journal*, Delhi, 2011.

Nayak, Mohan Lalit and Pandey, Bijayalaxmi, "Female Foeticide in India: Some Observations", *Golden Research Thoughts*, Vol. 1, 2012.

Srivastava, S.P., "The Perils of Pre-Birth Murder: A Sociological Analysis of Female Foeticide", *Journal of Social Welfare*, Vol. 47, No. 10, January 2001.

Visaria, L. Leela, "The Declining Sex Ratio in India", *National Media Journal India*, 2004.

Websites and Web Addresses

http://en.wikipedia.org/wiki/Save_girls, last visited on 18th March, 2013.

http://indialawyers.wordpress.com/category/female-foeticide, last visited on 17th March, 2013.

http://mistersingh.wordpress.com/2011/04/01/census-2011-trends-in-the-female-to-male-sex-ratio, last visited on 2nd March, 2013.

http://symlaw.spiggi.com/wp-content/uploads/2006/08/pndt_report.pdf, last visited on 16th January, 2013.

http://wcd.nic.in/KSY/ksyintro.htm, last visited on 17th March, 2013.

http://www.dailymail.co.uk/news/article-393896/Genocide-

Indiasdaughters.html, last visited on 25th January, 2013.

http://www.education.gov.uk/childrenandyoungpeople/healthandwellbeing/b0074766/uncrc, last visited on 13th April, 2013.

http://www.eldis.org/fulltext/*Preventive_Measures_For_Female_Foeticide*.pdf, last visited on 21st February, 2013.

http://www.hsph.harvard.edu/Organizations/healthnet/SAsia/forums/foeticide/articles/foeticide.html, last visited on 1st April, 2013.

http://www.indiatribune.com/index.php?option=com_content&view=article&id=8870:the-menace-of-female-foeticide-gujarats-initiatives&catid=107:coverpage&Itemid=471, last visited on 16th March, 2013.

http://www.medindia.net/health_statistics/general/sex-ratio-in-india-2011.asp, last visited on 21st February, 2013.

http://www.studymode.com/essays/Female-Foeticide-377153.html, last visited on 9th February, 2013.

http://www.thehindu.com/news/states/tamil-nadu/article2290679.ece, last visited on 18th April, 2013.

www.findlaw.com

www.indianexpress.com

www.indiankanoon.org

www.lawkhoj.com

www.legalserviceindia.com

www.manupatra.com

www.ndtv.com

www.punjabkesari.com

www.supreme courtus.gov

www.supremecourtofindia.nic.in

www.timesofindia.com

www.vakilno.1.com

www.westlaw.com

www.wikipedia.com

www.indiankanoon.com

www.scconline.com

Index

Index